INFLATION

Madhusudhanan S worked extensively as an economic consultant with the Government of India in New Delhi. He has a vast, multifunctional reserve of experience of around 16 years across multiple domains of economics.

His scholarly contributions have been noteworthy, including his article titled 'Rate of Interest and Indian Financial System', published in 2015 as a separate chapter in an edited book, *Financial Crisis and Indian Economy*. More recently, another article of his, 'Role of Monetary Policy during Financial Crisis and Its Impact in India', featured as a separate chapter in another edited book, *New Innovations in Economics, Business and Management Vol. 10*.

With his profound knowledge and practical experience, he offers readers a fresh perspective on economic issues—particularly inflation—in his latest work. His commitment to simplifying complex economic concepts makes his writing accessible to policymakers, students and general readers alike.

INFLATION

An Economic Phenomenon
That Matters

Madhusudhanan S

Published by
Rupa Publications India Pvt. Ltd 2025
7/16, Ansari Road, Daryaganj
New Delhi 110002

Sales centres:
Bengaluru Chennai
Hyderabad Jaipur Kathmandu
Kolkata Mumbai Prayagraj

Copyright © Madhusudhanan S 2025

The views and opinions expressed in this book are the author's own and the facts are as reported by him; these have been verified to the extent possible, and the publishers are not in any way liable for the same.

All rights reserved.
No part of this publication may be reproduced, transmitted, or stored in a retrieval system, in any form or by any means, electronic, mechanical, photocopying, recording or otherwise, without the prior permission of the publisher.

P-ISBN: 978-93-6156-020-0
E-ISBN: 978-93-6156-694-3

First impression 2025

10 9 8 7 6 5 4 3 2 1

The moral right of the author has been asserted.

Printed in India

This book is sold subject to the condition that it shall not, by way of trade or otherwise, be lent, resold, hired out, or otherwise circulated, without the publisher's prior consent, in any form of binding or cover other than that in which it is published.

To my late grandparents and my late father, without whom I would not be what I am today. To my late brother Vasudevan S, who instilled faith in me from a young age. To my mother and uncle, without whose love and unwavering support this journey would not be possible. In addition, to Mr S. Prakash, who believed in me even when I doubted myself.
This book is dedicated to you.

Contents

Author's Note — ix

Part A
Inflation: Causes, Measures and Policies

1. What Is Inflation? The Causes and Effects of Inflation — 3
2. Different Types of Inflation, Measures, and How It Is Calculated — 14
3. Money Inflation vs. Price Inflation, and Hyperinflation — 25
4. Inflation and Economic Growth — 38
5. Inflation and the Stock Market — 51
6. Inflation and Fiscal Policy — 61
7. Measures to Control Inflation — 69

Part B
India, Inflation and Monetary Phenomena

8. The History and the Present Scenario of Inflation in India — 77
9. Inflation Expectations — 89
10. Inflation Targeting — 106

11. Monetary Policy and Inflation Targeting in India	117
12. Is Inflation Always and Everywhere a Monetary Phenomenon, and Is It Applicable to India?	130

Annexures

Annexure I	143
Annexure II	145
Annexure III	146
Annexure IV	149
Annexure V	155
Annexure VI	157
Annexure VII	165
Annexure VIII	167
Glossary	169
Acknowledgements	175
Endnotes	176
Bibliography	179
Index	185

Author's Note

In 2020, due to Covid-19, there was a global lockdown which caused a drop in demand as well as supply disruptions across the world. When the global lockdown and restrictions were lifted, there was a surge in demand, but due to the supply disruptions, the economy couldn't meet this surge. This led to a unique kind of inflation in the post-pandemic period. The threat of this looming crisis hovered over the global economy for almost two years.

For centuries, the ghosts of past inflations have left behind lessons and opportunities for learning. Still, at present, inflation remains a threat to many economies throughout the world. This necessitates a deeper and more thorough understanding of the subject before policymakers and analysts go for a wider and more intense analysis.

Inflation is an economic phenomenon that matters to every person. It has a profound impact on consumers, investors and the economy as a whole. This book tries to explain these impacts lucidly.

The book is divided into Part A and Part B. Part A discusses inflation, its causes, and various measures and policies to deal with it, and Part B focuses on the themes of inflation and monetary phenomena in general.

Part A of the book consists of seven chapters. Chapter 1 defines inflation, its causes and its effects. Inflation is defined as a constant increase in the general price level of goods and services in an economy over a period of time. It erodes purchasing power. The relationship between demand and supply is one of the key drivers of inflation. A moderate level of inflation is known to be good for economic growth, while high levels, or hyperinflation, impacts the economy badly.

Deflation, which is the opposite of inflation, means a sustained decrease in the general price level. It leads to a decline in consumer spending, which may result in economic stagnation.

Inflation plays a vital role in economic policymaking. It is pertinent to understand inflation not only for policymakers, but also for businesses and individuals; this is because inflation influences investment decisions, interest rates and government policies.

There are different types of inflation. When demand exceeds supply, prices increase. This is known as demand-pull inflation. Factors like changes in government policies, increases in production costs, fluctuations in exchange rates, and global economic conditions also influence inflation.

An increase in the cost of production can lead to an increase in the prices of goods and services. This kind of inflation is known as cost-push inflation. When inflation expectations are high, and consumers and businesses adjust their behaviour accordingly, it is known as built-in inflation.

The traditional definition of inflation characterizes it as an increase in the money supply. However, today it is referred to as an increase in general price levels. Chapter 3 talks about monetary and price inflation.

What is the link between inflation and economic growth? Inflation results in a decline in purchasing power, which eventually lowers the GDP. While this may give the impression that the GDP and inflation are negatively correlated, there are research findings that have demonstrated a positive correlation between the two (Chapter 4).

Inflation also has an impact on the stock market (Chapter 5). It mainly depends on the central bank's monetary policy decisions and the investor's ability to hedge.

The government is more responsible for the fiscal policy, which frequently has a political goal. It is also significant to comprehend how inflation impacts the economy's budget. This is discussed in Chapter 6.

Every economy should control inflation, and it has to implement appropriate measures to do this (Chapter 7). There are various measures to control inflation, deploying various economic policies such as monetary and fiscal ones.

Chapter 8 discusses the history of inflation in India since the 1950s. It also sheds light on the present scenario.

Actual inflation is greatly influenced by inflation expectations (Chapter 9). These are determined by the central bank's ability to maintain price stability. Inflation expectations are essential for monetary policies to be implemented effectively.

These days, monetary policies are implemented more effectively with inflation targets. Inflation targeting is a global phenomenon which has taken an important place in the policymaking of many economies across the world (Chapter 10). For this reason, many economists favour it.

Similarly, the monetary policy is important in every economy. It is considered one of the main policy frameworks to attack inflation. Chapter 11 discusses the evolution of the monetary policy in India and how inflation targeting, by being a part of it, has become a tool to control inflation.

The famous monetarist Milton Friedman stated, 'Inflation is always and everywhere a monetary phenomenon.' This statement needed further examination, which has been carried out by many researchers in the recent past. They have subsequently challenged the statement. So, is inflation a monetary phenomenon? This is discussed in the last chapter of this book.

To sum up, inflation is a complex phenomenon that calls for a deeper understanding in order to handle it with care. In this book, we learn not only about the causes, effects, different types and policy implications of inflation, but also about the evolution of inflation and monetary policies in India. We also get to understand inflation targeting in India and other economies. I hope and believe this book will stimulate your interest and inspire you to do more research on the subject.

One may think there are many books on inflation. Then how is this book going to be different from the others? Well, the answer lies in one's interest in the subject. To explain with an example, there are many brands of outfits and jewellery available in the market, but only a few brands keep acquiring new customers. In the same way, a person who has a thirst to learn about the subject of inflation will at least find some new insights in this book.

Inflation is a topic which has inspired me since my

college days. I have read many books on it, and it motivated me to write a book which would be precise and written in a simple language so that even the common man is able to understand it. I feel that having more than fifteen years of experience as an economic researcher who has explored various topics, including inflation, makes me a little qualified to have a say on this subject.

I have made sure, to a great extent, to keep the use of terminology from economics to a minimum, so that anyone who reads this book can understand everything clearly. I hope the readers like it.

Madhusudhanan S
2024

Part A

Inflation: Causes, Measures and Policies

1

What Is Inflation? The Causes and Effects of Inflation

Inflation is when too much money chases too few goods and services.

—Harold Trevor Colbourn

Inflation, inflation, inflation—we have heard this term more and more often in the past three years, especially after the pandemic (i.e. Covid-19). Due to the global lockdown and restrictions, there was a decline in demand. And also, there were supply disruptions across the world.

As the lockdown and restrictions were lifted, there was a surge in demand. However, due to supply disruptions, the economy couldn't meet this sudden surge. This led to an inflation in the post-pandemic period.

Inflation has become a global phenomenon, with almost every economy experiencing higher levels of it. Food and energy prices are the main drivers of this high inflation. In many economies, the core inflation[1] (i.e. excluding food and energy prices) still remains high. The surge in inflation is connected to many factors. Global supply chain disruptions during the pandemic, the war in Ukraine, and unrest in other parts of the world have contributed in worsening the food and energy shortages.

The surge in inflation, thus, is not only due to the price of oil and other commodities, but also due to domestic factors which have played a crucial role in recent inflations.

Currently, inflation poses a threat to many economies around the world. It has become a serious and pressing issue. Therefore, it is pertinent to have a better and more in-depth understanding of the subject for policymakers and analysts before they carry on with a detailed analysis and suggest policy measures. Inflation affects consumers, investors, and the economy as a whole. To everyone's surprise, while the idea generates the most discussion nowadays, it still remains highly misunderstood.

In a layperson's language, inflation denotes an ongoing rise in the general price levels in an economy. Economically, the rate of increase in the price level of goods and services over a given period of time is called inflation. To simplify, it is an overall increase in the price level of goods and services in an economy or a country over a period of time, and is often expressed in percentages.

Here are two important points to note which will help us understand inflation better:

1. When the inflation rate decreases (it is called disinflation), it refers to the rate at which the price level has gone down—not the prices themselves.
2. Inflation is an increase in the average level of prices—but not all the prices in the economy increase.

When inflation increases, purchasing power (or the value of the currency or money) declines. Economists are of the view that inflation occurs when the growth of money supply exceeds economic growth.

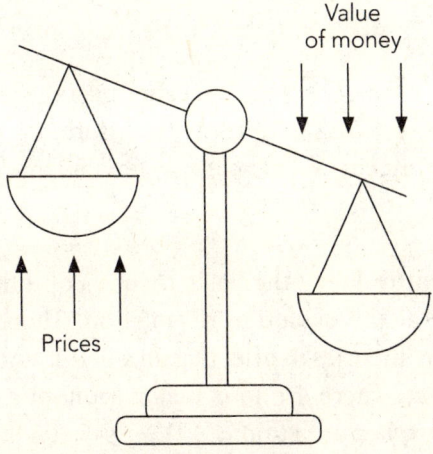

The term 'inflation' was first used to refer to the condition of the currency and later to the condition of money, and it now describes prices. The evolution or the shift in the meaning was inevitable. And while describing inflation as a condition of 'too much money', naturally the question arises: How much money is too much money? The quantity theory of money (which we will discuss in detail later) comes to the rescue with a solution, stating that too much money is an increase in the money stock, which comes along with an increase in the general price level. In other words, an increase in the money supply affects the general price level.

On the other hand, the Keynesians challenged the direct link between money and the price level, resulting in a shift in perspective, where inflation was primarily associated with a general increase in prices rather than a direct consequence of monetary factors. If it is not linked to the money supply, any price rise can be legitimately called inflation.

> ### DO YOU KNOW?
>
> The term 'inflation' is from the Latin 'inflate', meaning 'to blow up or inflate', and it was first used in a monetary sense to describe 'an increase in the amount of money' in 1838.

It is pertinent to know the basic theories of inflation as we have a look at the evolution of inflation. Therefore, let us delve into the theories in brief to gain a better understanding of the subject. There are four major economic theories to define and explain inflation.

1. The Quantity Theory of Money

The first and oldest theory of inflation is the quantity theory of money. It was originally articulated in 1517 by a mathematician called Nicolaus Copernicus. The theory was revived by David Hume in the eighteenth century. Then it was refined by a group of economists at the University of Chicago, under the leadership of Milton Friedman.

This theory opines that inflation is mainly a 'monetary' occurrence. It argues that inflation is determined by the money supply in the economy. An increase in the money supply (or the circulation of money) is directly proportional to an increase in the price of goods and services over time.

2. The Demand-Pull Theory of Inflation

This theory states that when the cost of goods and services rises, demand becomes greater than the available supply, which, in turn, increases the prices (or say, causes inflation). In simple terms, when demand increases with limited supply, prices increase to meet the demand. Hence, this theory is called demand-pull inflation.

John Maynard Keynes's theory of economics claims that the aggregate demand influences both inflation and output. One of Keynes's aims for devising this theory was to pull the economy out of recession on its own. The famous quote, or the common definition of inflation, 'Too much money chasing too few goods' summarizes this theory.

3. The Cost-Push Theory

The cost-push theory states that inflation is a result of a rise in the cost of production—irrespective of whether it is raw materials or wages. The theory assumes that the prices of goods are determined mainly by their cost of production. The manufacturer may transfer the extra costs—due to the rise in input costs—to consumers, by increasing the prices of goods. Hence, the theory is known as the cost-push theory.

4. The Structural Theory of Inflation

According to this theory, inflation is caused by a structural weakness in a country's ability to produce goods or maintain an adequate flow of supply. This type of inflation more often prevails in developing economies. Inefficient supply chains, poor infrastructure or outdated technologies may be the reasons for underproductivity. This creates an imbalance in demand and supply, and leads to inflation. This cannot be easily handled by a change in the monetary policy as the inflation stems from structural issues.

From the above theories, one can perceive that the matter of concern isn't just the presence of inflation, but that expectations and perceptions also play a vital role. The mere expectation of inflation can also increase demand. Therefore, inflation cannot fall under only one of these categories—it may fall under a combination thereof. Sometimes, the reasons may not be certain.

From the evolution and the basic theories of inflation, we will now move to what causes it. The causes or drivers of inflation arise from the crux of these theories.

The Causes or Drivers of Inflation

There is a famous classical saying on inflation: 'inflation is a situation when too much money chases too few goods and services'. This maintains that inflation is when the quantity of money in circulation exceeds the goods and services available in the economy. Classical economists state that sustained inflation is due to greater money supply in the economy.

Therefore, the root cause of inflation is an increase in the money supply. This increase in the money supply of an economy is facilitated through different mechanisms, for example, i) printing money, ii) officially (legally) devaluing the currency, iii) raising wages, and such others. Whatever the mechanism by which it is carried through, it results in a decline in the purchasing power within the economy.

A recent International Monetary Fund (IMF) study (2024) claims that the main drivers of inflation are oil prices and demand. This study, which was conducted by the World

Bank, attempted the first systematic empirical analysis of the drivers of global inflation for the past 32 years, in the period between 1970 and 2022. It found that 38 per cent of global inflation contributions came from oil price shocks, and around 28 per cent came from global demand shocks over the past five decades. The contributions of global supply shocks and interest rate shocks to global inflation were much smaller, according to this study.

> DO YOU KNOW?
>
> The inflation rate for consumer prices in India moved, over the past 61 years, between 7.6 per cent and 28.6 per cent. Overall, the price increase was 8,698.14 per cent. Thus, an item that cost ₹100 in 1960 costs ₹8,798.14 in the beginning of 2024.

Other than these, there are a few other causes of inflation. These are as follows:

1. Increase in Public Spending

One of the most important elements of total spending in an economy is government spending. As government spending increases, it invariably triggers an increase in aggregate demand, and as the money supply increases, this may lead to inflationary pressures in the economy (this is especially applicable in less developed countries).

2. Population Growth

This may sound absurd to a few economists, but the truth is that population growth is also a cause of inflation. When the population of an economy grows, the total demand increases, and this leads to inflation.

3. Hoarding

This is a moral issue, as well as a cause of inflation. When sellers or producers stock their commodities and do not bring them to the market, it is called hoarding. This creates an artificial demand in the economy and ultimately leads to inflation.

4. Supply Chain Issues

When the free flow of materials and products is affected, it is known as a supply chain problem or disruption. This leads to inflation. This is one of the most common problems which the entire world faces. It has also been one of the causes of inflation in recent times, especially during the Covid-19 pandemic.

5. Genuine Shortage of Factors of Production

When any of the factors of production is in short supply, it affects production. This is a genuine shortage and it leads to inflation.

6. Increase in Indirect Taxes

As taxes are the primary sources of revenue for governments, sometimes they impose or increase indirect taxes on businesses, such as excise duty, VAT, GST, and others, in order to increase their revenue. This imposition or increase in indirect taxes is reflected in the final price of the commodities as they are passed on to the consumer. This leads to inflation.

7. Natural Calamities

Inflation may take place due to natural calamities like floods which may spoil crops. This reduces the supply of agricultural produce and leads to an increase in the prices of commodities.

The Triggers or Circumstances Leading to Inflation

There are some common circumstances which lead to inflation:

1. Careless Monetary Policy

High inflation for a prolonged period may happen due to laxity or a careless monetary policy. When the money supply increases beyond the size of the economy, the value of the currency diminishes. In other words, there is a fall in purchasing power within the economy, and this leads to inflation. This relationship between the size of the economy and the money supply is called the quantity theory of money, which is one of the oldest economic hypotheses.

2. Government Deficit

When the expenditure of the government exceeds its revenue, it is known as a fiscal deficit. Many times, the government opts for borrowing or printing new currency to finance this deficit. This increases the money supply and leads to inflation.

3. Supply and Demand Shocks

When there is pressure on the supply or demand side of the economy, it may also lead to inflation. When there is a supply shock, it disturbs production—for example, if there is an increase in oil prices, it can increase the costs of production or reduce overall supply, which leads to cost-push inflation. When demand increases and exceeds the production capacity of an economy, it results in demand-pull inflation.

The Effects of Inflation on the Economy

1. **Market Instability:** If there is unpredictable inflation expectations, then it affects the overall economy and leads to market instability; this goes on to affect the investment plans of companies.
2. **Purchasing Power:** An increase in the inflation rate leads to a decrease in purchasing power. Due to inflation, the value of money decreases.
3. **Inequality:** As money loses its value, the predominantly low-income groups of the population spend a greater percentage of their income and save less money (or they don't have any money to save). In other words, inflation usually takes up most of their income.
4. **Exchange Rates:** When the inflation rate increases, domestic products become less competitive within the economy, which can weaken the domestic currency. This leads to a decline in the exchange rate. When there is a decline in the exchange rate, it can lead to cost-push inflation.
5. **Boosts Spending and Investment:** During inflationary periods, as the value of money depreciates, the consumer often tends to spend more. Due to the fear of inflation expectations, consumers often spend more before the value of money goes further down. Investors invest in

gold, bonds and other forms of investment to offset the losses incurred during inflation.

6. **Economic Growth:** Inflation can also lead to short-term economic growth, as it implies an increase in the aggregate demand.
7. **Interest Rates:** Inflation and interest rates have a direct relationship. So whenever inflation increases, interest rates are increased to control it.
8. **Reduces Employment:** Due to inflation, interest rates are increased, and this discourages investors from investing more. Therefore, it may be reflected in a reduction in employment opportunities.

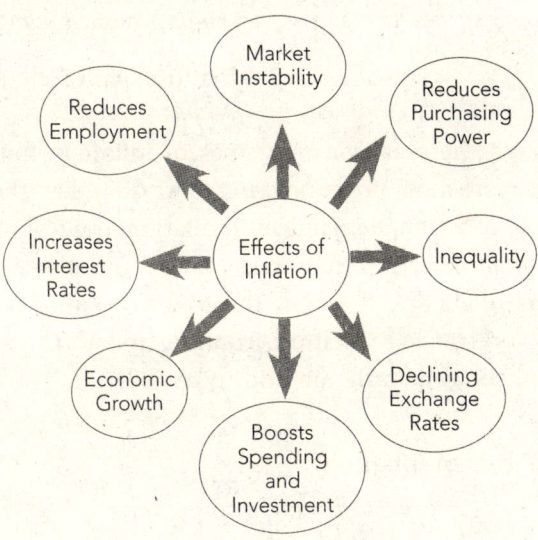

2

Different Types of Inflation, Measures, and How It Is Calculated

Nothing so weakens the government as persistent inflation.

—John Kenneth Galbraith

Though there are various types of inflation, four main types are more prominent in the world today. These are: cost-push inflation, demand-pull inflation, built-in inflation and stagflation. Other than these, inflation is also classified in terms of its speed levels; these are creeping inflation, walking or trotting inflation, running inflation, galloping inflation, runaway inflation and hyperinflation.

Major Types of Inflation

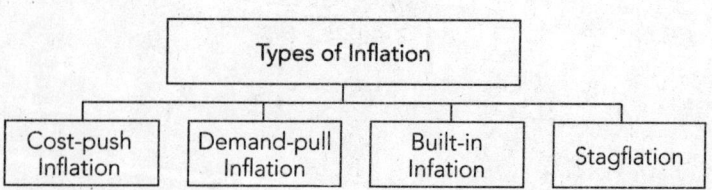

1. Cost-push Inflation

When the cost of inputs (raw materials, transportation, and others) increases, the price of the product naturally also increases. This increase in inflation is called cost-push inflation. The increase in energy prices and commodity prices which are passed on to consumers is an example of cost-push inflation.

This can be explained via a chart or a diagram. This example is applicable mainly in the short run. The diagram given below depicts the movement of the aggregate supply (AS) from AS to AS1, due to an increase in the cost of the inputs. As the aggregate supply moves from P to P1, the aggregate demand of the economy moves from AD to AD1. This results in a decrease in the real gross domestic product (GDP).

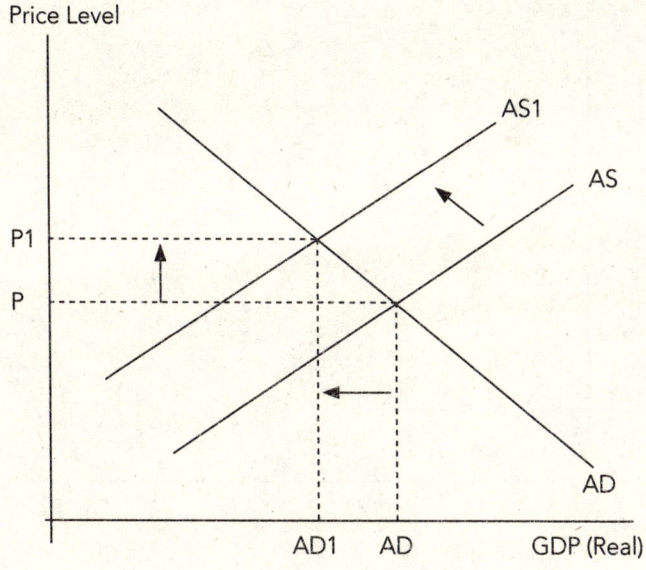

Chart 1: Cost-Push Inflation

2. Demand-pull Inflation

When the money supply increases, the aggregate demand for goods and services also increases. When the aggregate demand increases more rapidly than the economy's production capacity, it leads to inflation. This is called demand-pull inflation and can be explained via a chart or a diagram. This example is applicable only when the economy is facing mild inflation (or creeping inflation).

The diagram given below depicts the movement of the aggregate demand (AD) from AD to AD1 due to inflation expectations. As price levels move from P to P1, the aggregate demand of the economy moves from D to D1. This results in an increase in the real GDP.

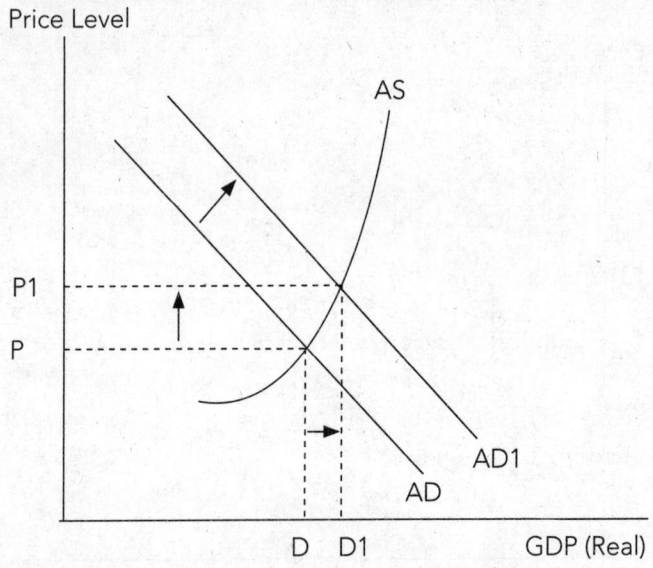

Chart 2: Demand-Pull Inflation

3. Built-in Inflation

The inflation that occurs due to inflation expectations is called built-in inflation. When there is inflation, people may expect a continuous increase in the prices of goods and services in the future at the same rate. So labour will demand an increase in wages to maintain their standard of living. Thus, when wages are raised, there is an increase in the cost of production which results in a rise in the prices of goods and services (i.e. inflation). In other words, when the cost of production increases, it is passed on to the consumer through increases in the prices of the products.

Built-in inflation is a combination of both cost-push and demand-pull inflation. When there is an increase in wages, there is more disposable income for consumers which increases the aggregate consumption and aggregate demand.

4. Stagflation

Many economists may not accept stagflation as a type of inflation, though it is one. Stagflation is a situation where there is slow economic growth, high unemployment, as well as inflation. In simple terms, when economic growth is stagnant but inflation still prevails, it is called stagflation.

Once, it was believed that it was impossible for stagflation to occur. But it has occurred repeatedly across the world since the 1970s. It is a combination of recession and inflation.

> **DO YOU KNOW?**
>
> The term 'stagflation' was first used by British politician Iain Macleod in a speech before the House of Commons in 1965, a time of economic stress in the United Kingdom. He called the combined effects of inflation and stagnation a 'stagflation situation'.

Types of Inflation by the Rate of Increase or Speed Levels

1. Creeping Inflation (1%–4%)

Creeping inflation is inflation which increases slowly over a period of time. It is also called mild inflation. This inflation is not immediately noticeable. The range of creeping inflation is from one per cent to four per cent. Many economists accept that this kind of inflation is very useful for economic growth.

2. Walking Inflation (2%–10%)

Walking inflation is also called moderate or trotting inflation. This is harmful as it hits the cycle of supply and demand. People tend to buy more and more to beat future inflation (expectations), and this ultimately affects the supply. When inflation is in single digits, it is not a problem (especially when it is below 10 per cent). But when inflation rises over four per cent, the central banks of the economy are more concerned about it.

3. Running Inflation (10%–20%)

Many economists combine running inflation with galloping inflation, but there is a difference between the two. When inflation rates are anywhere between 10 and 20 per cent, it is called running inflation. In other words, when there is a significant increase in the inflation rate, it is running inflation. This level of inflation is a cause for greater alarm, and is more problematic for the economy because any policy measure may lead the inflation to creep higher.

4. Galloping Inflation (20%–100%)

Galloping inflation is a serious problem, and it is highly challenging to bring it under control. When the inflation rate is from 20 to 100 per cent, it is called galloping inflation. This is also known as jumping inflation. At this point, the value of money diminishes faster and the economy is in danger. The economy becomes unstable and the government loses credibility during galloping inflation. Therefore, it must be prevented at any cost.

There is no universally agreed-upon range, when it comes to galloping inflation. However, Paul A. Samuelson confined its range to 200 per cent annually.

5. Hyperinflation (>1,000%)

This is also called runaway inflation because the value of money declines rapidly. When inflation occurs at a rate of more than 50 per cent per month, or 1,000 per cent a year, it is called hyperinflation. In case of this inflation, the prices keep changing even faster and it becomes a daily occurrence. Though this is a very rare situation, there are a few examples of hyperinflation in history. These are: Germany in 1923,

Zimbabwe in 2008–09 (started in November 2008), and Venezuela in 2018.

These are the various types of inflation classified on the basis of the rate of increase. Other than these, there are a few more types and situations of inflation:

Deflation

When the general price levels decline below zero per cent, it is called deflation. This is also called negative inflation. In this situation, purchasing power increases, i.e. people can buy more with less money. This situation is not good for the economy because investors stop investing and unemployment starts increasing. Deflation should never be confused with disinflation.

Disinflation

Disinflation is defined as a decrease in the rate of inflation. Disinflation is a situation where the inflation rate is slowing down, but is not negative (positive). In other words, the rate of increase in price levels is slowing down compared to what it had been.

Wage-push Inflation

As the name denotes, this is when the prices of the final products increase due to an increase in wages. Inflation which occurs due to an increase in wages is thus called wage-push inflation.

Imported Inflation

Inflation occurs due to a depreciation in the value of the currency. When a currency depreciates, imports become expensive, which increases the prices in the domestic market. This depreciation also makes exports more competitive and leads to an increase in the aggregate demand.

Open Inflation

When inflation is determined by demand and supply in the market, it is called open inflation. In other words, inflation is determined by the market. In this type of inflation, the value of money does not decrease. When inflation is determined by market forces, the government and the monetary authorities of the country do not take any measures to control it.

Suppressed Inflation

In this situation, the aggregate demand is greater than the aggregate supply, but the government does not allow the prices to rise. In other words, inflation is suppressed or managed by the government. This mostly occurs in a controlled economy.

Shrinkflation

In this type of inflation, the prices of the products may be the same but the sizes of products are reduced.

Structural Inflation

Inflation also occurs due to structural problems. For example, infrastructural bottlenecks may cause inflation.

Types of Price Indices—Measures of Inflation

There are various measures of inflation. But mainly, inflation is measured in three ways. These are: the producer price index (PPI), the wholesale price index (WPI), and the consumer price index (CPI) (also known as the retailer price index).

1. Producer Price Index (PPI)

Inflation measured at the producer level is called the producer price index (PPI). The average change in selling prices received by domestic producers of intermediate goods and services over a period of time is called the producer price index. This measure of inflation is from the producer's perspective.

2. Wholesale Price Index (WPI)

The wholesale price index (WPI) is a measure of inflation which captures the inflation movement of wholesalers. It captures the movement of price changes at the wholesale level.

3. Consumer Price Index (CPI)

The consumer price index (CPI) is a measure of inflation at retail prices or at the consumer level. It is also called retail inflation as it collects the prices quoted by retailers.

Different Types of Inflation

A few other measures of inflation are:

Core Inflation

One of the major measures of inflation, core inflation excludes volatile factors such as food and energy prices. This makes core inflation more constant. Policymakers look at not only CPI (all-India or combined) but also core inflation to make policy decisions. Core inflation is considered one of the best indicators of inflation for making policy decisions.

Personal Consumption Expenditures (PCE) Price Index

The PCE is different from the CPI, as this price index captures changes in the prices of all consumption items and not just of those paid out of the pockets of consumers (like CPI). It is known for capturing inflation in terms of a wide range of consumer expenditures, along with reflecting changes in consumer behaviour. The USA covers this index.

Harmonized Index of Consumer Prices (HICP)

This index prevails across the European Union (EU) countries. The HICP is the consumer price inflation in the EU countries. The methodology is harmonized across all the EU countries, to compare with data from other countries.

How Inflation Is Calculated

Many countries use the CPI as their benchmark measure to calculate inflation, using it for their policy measures. The formulae to derive the inflation rate from the consumer price index are as follows:

$$\text{Inflation Rate} = \frac{\text{CPI}_{\text{Current Year}} - \text{CPI}_{\text{Last Year}}}{\text{CPI}_{\text{Last Year}}} \times 100 - 100$$

Or,

$$\text{Inflation Rate} = \frac{\text{CPI}_{\text{Current Year}}}{\text{CPI}_{\text{Last Year}}} \times 100 - 100$$

Remember, the CPI is an index. The above formula is to derive the inflation rate of the economy for a year (the same can be applied to calculate monthly data).

3

Money Inflation vs. Price Inflation, and Hyperinflation

Inflation is always and everywhere a monetary phenomenon...

—Milton Friedman

The definition of inflation changed over the course of the twentieth century. The original definition referred to an increase in the money supply, whereas today we define it as an increase in price levels. In this chapter, we will distinguish between monetary and price inflation. Milton Friedman famously said, 'Inflation is always and everywhere a monetary phenomenon in the sense that it is and can be produced only by a more rapid increase in the quantity of money than in output.' This is because, most of the time, a rapid increase in price levels goes hand in hand with rapid monetary expansion.

The increase in bank lending or fiscal deficit (due to increased government spending) will result in inflation—this inflation is known as monetary inflation. This includes both physical and digital money in the economy. The increase in the money supply will result in faster economic growth and consumer price inflation. The reason for this increase in the price levels (following an increase in the money supply) is more money chasing fewer goods (actually the same number of goods—as supply cannot be increased in the short term). What comes first, price inflation or monetary inflation? This will be seen later in this chapter.

The famous Austrian economist Ludwig von Mises, in his book *Economic Freedom and Interventionism* (which was a part of his speech in 1951), stated:

> There is nowadays a very reprehensible, even dangerous, semantic confusion that makes it extremely difficult for the non-expert to grasp the true state of affairs. Inflation, as this term was always used everywhere and especially in this country, means increasing the quantity of money and bank notes in circulation and the quantity of bank deposits subject to check. But people today use the term 'inflation' to refer to the phenomenon that is an inevitable consequence of inflation, that is the tendency of all prices and wage rates to rise.

Ludwig von Mises goes on to explain how the term has deviated from its original meaning of monetary inflation to mean price inflation:

> The result of this deplorable confusion is that there is no term left to signify the cause of this rise in prices and wages. There is no longer any word available to signify the phenomenon that has been, up to now, called inflation. It follows that nobody cares about inflation in the traditional sense of the term. As you

> cannot talk about something that has no name, you cannot fight it. Those who pretend to fight inflation are in fact only fighting what is the inevitable consequence of inflation, rising prices...

We will read the remaining lines later in this chapter.

This statement by Ludwig von Mises clearly shows the difference between monetary inflation and price inflation. The rapid increase in price levels goes hand in hand with rapid monetary expansion. When there is genuine hyperinflation, it means that the government is printing more money than usual.

> **DO YOU KNOW?**
>
> 28 hyperinflations occurred in the twentieth century, with 20 happening after 1980.

In the twentieth century, many economies experienced hyperinflation. There are many historical records or examples of the same. Here are six famous examples of hyperinflation:

1. The German Hyperinflation (1921–23)

The most famous inflation in recent history is Germany's hyperinflation from 1921 to 1923, after the First World War. However, this was not the worst case of all (we will read about the worst one next).

The inflation in Germany doubled during the First World War. However, this was just the beginning of the country's economic troubles. After the end of the First World War, the Weimar government was bound by the

Treaty of Versailles. According to this treaty, the Weimar Republic could never wage war on its neighbours again. Along with this, the treaty had harsh terms on reparation payments to the Allies. During the War billions of marks (the German currency then) were hoarded, and they suddenly came back in circulation. This added to the Weimar government's massive debt problems. To pay their debts, the government resorted to printing more money.

The Weimar government went on printing money, from millions of marks to trillions. The exchange rate of the German mark was 4.2 to \$1 in 1914, but after nine years, i.e. in 1923, it became 4.2 trillion to \$1. In August 1924, a new currency called the rentenmark was introduced in Germany. It took a trillion old marks to get one new rentenmark. Due to the introduction of the new currency, prices were stabilized—as only a limited number of notes were printed. This also meant that there was a rise in the value of the currency. This helped the German economy restore confidence within the nation, as well as across the globe, and ended the German hyperinflation.

2. The Hungary Hyperinflation (1945–46)

The worst inflation ever in the history of inflation was the one in Hungary in 1945–46. Hyperinflation is not a new thing in Hungary. After the First World War, Hungary's government went for printing money to fill its budget deficit. The exchange rate before the First World War was five kronen to \$1. This changed to 70,000 kronen to \$1 after the War. Hungary introduced a new currency called pengö in 1926, replacing the kronen. The new exchange rate was 12,500 pengö to \$1. The number of bank notes in circulation by the end of the month, from July 1945 to July 1946, are as follows:

Table 1
Number of Bank Notes in Circulation—End of Month

July 1945	25,433,900.000
August 1945	35,521,100.000
September 1945	51,034,100.000
October 1945	115,961,100.000
November 1945	364,592,000.000
December 1945	765,446,300.000
January 1946	1,646,450,000.000
February 1946	5,237,808,300.000
March 1946	34,001,636,300.000
April 1946	434,304,091,200.000
May 1946	65,588,977,992,200.000
June 1946	6,277,271,200,000,000,000.000
July 1946	47,300,000,000,000,000,000,000.000

Source: Adapted from Siklos (Appendix on page 215–216) (1991), and Nagaro (1948)

During the Second World War, most of Europe's industrial capacity (approximately 90 per cent) was damaged. After the War, due to the destruction of the production capacity, prices started rising in Hungary. There was no tax to rely upon, so the government went for printing money to stimulate the economy. The government literally flooded the country with money to bring the economy back to normal again.

Hungary recorded the highest inflation ever in history between the end of 1945 and July 1946. The circulation of money went from 25 billion pengö to 47 septillion (i.e. trillion trillion) in July 1946. When inflation was at its peak, prices were rising at the rate of 150,000 per cent per day.

On 1 August 1946, Hungary replaced its currency, the pengö, with the forint. The rate of one forint was 400,000 quadrillion pengö. This stabilized the economy and the prices remained relatively stable.

DO YOU KNOW?

The US has never experienced hyperinflation. The inflation rate reached 23 per cent in 1920 and 14 per cent in 1980 (nowhere near the 50 per cent benchmark for hyperinflation). The government watches inflation rates closely. When necessary, the Federal Bank steps in to slow the rising inflation using monetary policy. Until recently, US inflation has averaged at about two per cent annually.

---

3. The Yugoslavia Hyperinflation (1992–94)

In the 1990s, one country came close but failed to beat Hungary's record in the inflation marathon, and that country was Yugoslavia. Yugoslavia's hyperinflation lasted 24 months from 1992 to 1994, and it was only two months shorter than the Russian hyperinflation of the 1920s. In early 1992, Yugoslavia disintegrated, and the new Federal Republic of Yugoslavia, formerly known as Serbia and Montenegro, was formed. Following the breakdown, the country's monthly hyperinflation would reach the benchmark of 50 per cent.

Its monthly inflation rate reached its peak at 313 million per cent in January 1994.

The United Nations sanctioned, or say imposed, an international trade restriction on the Federal Republic of Yugoslavia. This sanction impacted the GDP and the fiscal deficit of the economy. It increased from three per cent of GDP in 1990 to 28 per cent of GDP in 1993. The government chose to print money to revive the economy and fund the fiscal deficit, which resulted in a hyperinflation. The monetization started in 1991. The value of the currency was rapidly falling, and the currency officially collapsed on 6 January 1994. The Yugoslavian government declared the German mark as the new legal tender for all financial transactions in the country, including the payment of taxes.[2]

4. The Zimbabwe Hyperinflation (2007–08)

The most recent and severe hyperinflation occurred in Zimbabwe in 2007–08. This is the second most severe case of hyperinflation in history after the Hungarian hyperinflation. Prices increased more than 79 billion per cent, or 98 per cent, per day in November 2008.

External debt, as a share of the GDP, increased from 11 per cent in 1980 to 119 per cent in 2008. The economic troubles and hyperinflation eroded the wealth of the citizens and set the country back by more than half a century.[3] In 2009, the country adopted the dollar and it became the primary currency. In case of the hyperinflation in Zimbabwe, it was observed that the money supply and the prices were moving in tandem with each other (or say, moving parallelly).

Table 2
Zimbabwe's Hyperinflation

Date	Month-over-Month Inflation Rate (%)	Year-over-Year Inflation Rate (%)
March 2007	50.54	2,200.20
April 2007	100.70	3,713.90
May 2007	55.40	4,530.00
June 2007	86.20	7,251.10
July 2007	31.60	7,634.80
August 2007	11.80	6,592.80
September 2007	38.70	7,982.10
October 2007	135.62	14,840.65
November 2007	131.42	26,470.78
December 2007	240.06	66,212.30
January 2008	120.83	100,580.16
February 2008	125.86	164,900.29
March 2008	281.29	417,823.13
April 2008	212.54	650,599.00
May 2008	433.40	2,233,713.43
June 2008	839.30	11,268,758.90
July 2008	2,600.24	231,150,888.87
August 2008	3,190.00	9,690,000,000.00
September 2008	12,400.00	471,000,000,000.00
October 2008	690,000,000.00	3,840,000,000,000,000,000.00
14 November 2008	79,600,000,000.00	89,700,000,000,000,000,000,000.00

Notes: The Reserve Bank of Zimbabwe reported inflation rates for March 2007–July 2008. Steve Hanke and Alex K.F. Kwok calculated the rates for August 2008–14 November 2008.

Sources: The Reserve Bank of Zimbabwe (2008a), and Steve Hanke and Alex K.F. Kwok's calculations

5. The Civil War in the United States of America (1861–65)[4]

During the Civil War, the US witnessed high inflation in both the northern (Union) and the southern (Confederate) economies. However, the high inflation was particularly distinct in the Confederacy. The debt obligation of the federal government increased from $65 million in 1861 to $2.7 billion in 1865 (this included the issuance of notes by the treasury). The Northerners absorbed $700 million of the new currency when they bought treasury notes worth $2 billion.

It is estimated that over a third of the Confederate government's revenue or income came from the printing press, while only 11 per cent came from tax receipts (the rest were covered by floating bonds). This had a major impact on the economic stability of the Confederate states, and this was best visible in their price behaviour. There was a rapid increase in prices in the Confederate states. Consumer prices doubled from early 1861 to early 1862, and increased by a factor of 13 by the middle of 1863, which was near the start of the war. During the war, inflation in the Confederate states increased by 9,000 per cent.[5]

By the end of the war, with military defeats in 1864 and 1865, the value of the Confederate currency had become virtually zero. This made Southerners barter or use Union dollars (if they could find it). The Union also experienced inflation, though it was not nearly as bad as that in the Confederate states. The Union inflation increased by 75 per cent between 1861 and 1865. The inflation during the Civil War is the only phase in American history so far which falls under the definition of hyperinflation.

6. The Venezuela Inflation (2016–21)

One of the most recent cases of hyperinflation happened in Venezuela in 2016–21. Venezuela is still recovering from hyperinflation. The economy entered into hyperinflation in November 2016 due to excessive government spending and printing of money to control the high inflation rate. The economy faced political instability, economic problems, and foreign sanctions as a result of hyperinflation. The hyperinflation peaked at over 65,000 per cent in 2018. Then its recovery started in 2021.

The inflation rate was 274 per cent in 2016, 863 per cent in 2017, and 130,060 per cent in 2018. In 2019, it declined to 9,586 per cent. Three years later, the Central Bank of Venezuela accepted that the overall inflation rate had increased to 53,798,500 per cent between 2016 and 2019. In 2020, inflation declined to 2,959.8 per cent. From 2021, the decline in inflation started to accelerate, when it went down to 686.4 per cent the same year, with a further decline to 234.1 per cent in 2022. It came down to 189.8 per cent in 2023.

A noteworthy achievement in Venezuela's hyperinflation episode is that there was a significant decrease in money growth without structural changes in the economy's fiscal and monetary institutions, resulting in a sharp decline in inflation.

These were six instances where money inflation led to hyperinflation. In other words, hyperinflation sticks with the original definition of inflation.

Why Do Policies or Policymakers Fail to Stop or Address Inflation?

It is now time for us to read the remaining portion of Ludwig von Mises's quote:

> ...Their ventures are doomed to failure because they do not attack the root of the evil. They try to keep prices low while firmly committed to a policy of increasing the quantity of money that must necessarily make them soar. As long as this technological confusion is not entirely wiped out, there cannot be any question of stopping inflation.

Here, Ludwig von Mises clearly states that money inflation is the root cause of all inflationary problems, yet policymakers do not address this cause. Rather, they just try to keep the prices low. This automatically increases the money inflation and subsequently leads to an increase in prices (or say, price inflation).

A few other economists argue that hyperinflation occurs mainly due to an increase in expansionary fiscal policy, or say, an increase in the government's fiscal deficit. However, it is important to understand here that these fiscal deficits are funded either by borrowing from banks or by printing money. Therefore, again, they also come to have the same view, one way or the other. The examples of hyperinflation given above have proved the same thing.

What Comes First? Price Inflation or Monetary Inflation?

For those who advocate or point out that inflation is primarily due to an increase in the money supply, it is always argued that an increase in prices often occurs earlier than an increase in the money supply. This is not only true but also proved with the evidence of what happened in Korea after the outbreak of a war in the 1950s. During that time, the prices of raw materials started to increase because of the fear that they were going to be scarce. Manufacturers, as well as speculators, started to buy these raw materials to hold, to hoard for profit, or for their own inventories to protect themselves from scarcity. To do this, they had to borrow money from the banks; this rise in prices was accompanied by an equal rise in bank loans and deposits.[6] Therefore, in most cases, the increase in prices comes earlier, and is later accompanied by an increase in the money supply.

Monetary and Price Inflation

The term 'inflation' originally referred to an increase in the quantity of money, whereas these days it refers to an increase in prices. The connection between monetary inflation and price inflation is very powerful, making them inseparable. It has been witnessed that all cases of hyperinflation (see the above examples) involved both money and price inflation. Price inflation comes before monetary inflation.

A question may arise: if money inflation increases to a certain level, then will there be an increase in the price level (or price inflation) to the same extent? Well, the answer is, not necessarily. Monetary inflation may not always affect price inflation (but in most cases, it does). The best example of this is the quantitative easing during the financial crisis in the USA. This is because at that time the interest rate was zero and the US was in a liquidity trap.[7] (*See Annexure I*)

4

Inflation and Economic Growth

Inflation is not only unnecessary for economic growth.
As long as it exists it is the enemy of economic growth.

—Henry Hazlitt

The relationship between economic growth and inflation is a much-discussed and much-researched topic in the field of economics. Many economic theories have been formulated and a lot of research has been done on this over the years. Before going any further, it is important to understand the definition of economic growth.

Economic growth is an increase in the production of goods and services in an economy over a period of time, normally a year, and it is compared with that of the previous year. Economic growth is measured in both nominal and real terms (i.e., it is inflation-adjusted). It is normally defined as the gross domestic product (GDP).

Now, it is known that inflation means an increase in the price levels of goods and services. So, what is the relationship between inflation and economic growth?

When the price rises, purchasing power decreases, which ultimately lowers the GDP. Though it may look like there is a negative relationship between the GDP and inflation, there are also studies which have proved the existence of a positive relationship between the two. The Phillips curve is one of the best examples of this. It states that when there is constant high inflation, it reduces the unemployment rate and boosts economic growth.

There are many theories which talk about the relationship between inflation and growth. It is not possible to include all these theories in one single chapter, as even individually each theory is equal to one chapter of its own. Therefore, let us look at a few important theoretical views, one by one.

Theoretical Views on Growth and Inflation

Many economists, from classical to modern, have studied inflation and its impact on economic growth. This section discusses the main essence of these theories.

Classical Growth Theory

Adam Smith, the father of economics, recognized three factors of production, namely land, labour and capital. Smith advocated that the division of labour leads labourers towards specialization, which is the driver of growth. David Ricardo strengthened Adam Smith's theory of specialization and division of labour with his theory of comparative advantage. He stated that due to specialization, the economy has a comparative advantage and can trade with another one which can lead to greater economic growth.

The classical theories explained that capital accumulation and the reinvestment of profits which comes from specialization (due to the division of labour) gave the economy a comparative advantage, and as a result, there was some economic growth (or say, an increase in GDP). The classical theories never advocated any direct relationship between inflation and growth.

Keynesian Growth Theory

John Maynard Keynes wrote a book titled *The General Theory of Employment, Interest and Money* in 1936, and thereby established the foundation of the Keynesian theory. His theory was based on aggregate demand (AD) and aggregate supply (AS). Keynes believed that the government's expansion of economic policies would boost investment and increase demand to reach the full potential (or production capacity) of the economy. He believed in government intervention as he did not believe in a natural state of equilibrium. Keynes stated that when the economy was in recession or there was a downturn, it could not reach an equilibrium without government intervention.

To overcome the recession, Keynes proposed that the government spend more and cut taxes (or say, go for a deficit budget). This would increase consumer demand, lead to an increase in overall economic activity, and reduce unemployment.

The Quantity Theory of Money

In 1911, Irving Fisher, in his book *The Purchasing Power of Money*, explained the quantity theory of money. Fisher wrote: 'In short, the quantity theory asserts that (provided velocity of circulation and volume of trade are unchanged) if we increase the number of dollars, whether by renaming coins, or by debasing coins, or by increasing coinage, or by any other means, prices will be increased in the same proportion.'

This is one of the most important theories describing the relationship between money supply and inflation (including deflation). The theory states that there is a direct relationship between the money supply and the increase or decrease in price levels (i.e. inflation or deflation) in an economy.

In simple terms, it states that the money supply in an economy determines the price levels. That is, if there is an increase in the money supply, then there will be a proportional increase in price levels, and vice versa.

The quantity theory of money highlights the relationship between money supply and prices. The theory can be explained in terms of Irving Fisher's equation:

$$MV = PT$$

In the equation, **M** stands for total money supply, **V** stands for the velocity of circulation or money, **P** stands for the average or aggregate price level, and **T** stands for the total number of transactions.

According to this theory, prices are directly related to an increase in the money supply. Whenever there is an increase in T, the prices (i.e. P) will be constant—provided that there is a corresponding increase in the number of goods and services produced. But if there is no increase in the number of goods and services, then the prices (P) will increase.

In simple terms, a change in the money supply will affect the economy's production, prices and employment.

> ### DO YOU KNOW?
>
> Deflation doesn't mean the country is becoming poor. The economist A.C. Pigou argued that the market or the economy would do self-correction, and that during deflation, there might be an increase in GDP. This increase in GDP would slowly bring an economy out of deflation, or say, a liquidity trap.

The Monetarist Theory of Growth

This theory is famously known as monetarism. This theory was proposed by Milton Friedman. In his essay 'The Quantity Theory of Money—A Restatement', which was published in 1956, Friedman beautifully restated the old quantity theory of money. In his restatement, he said, 'Money does Matter.'

According to the monetarists, the money supply determined the price levels in an economy. Monetarism stated that when the money supply increased more or faster than the rate of growth of the national income, it was accompanied by inflation. It pointed out that the results would be different in the short run and in the long run.

According to the monetarists, the money supply had a greater influence on real GDP and employment (i.e. real variables) in the short run. In the long run, it had a greater impact on other nominal variables (but not real variables) and primarily the price level.

The Neo-Classical Growth Theory

Robert Solow and Trevor Swan first introduced the neo-classical theory in 1956. In their theory, they talked about the three driving forces of economic growth: namely labour, capital and technology. Their model or theory of growth was called the exogenous model or theory of growth. They argued that economic growth could not happen without technological changes or advances.

Robert Mundell and James Tobin, in their model (the Mundell-Tobin model), stated that inflation caused individuals to hold fewer money balances and go for other assets. They also stated that an increase in return on nominal assets would crowd out capital investment. The model stated that inflation caused an increase in real capital investment, which would lead to higher economic growth.

Alan C. Stockman presented a model[8] where capital and money growth were negatively related when a cash-in-advance constraint applied to both consumption and investment. He also stated that consumption alone was subject to the cash-in-advance constraint, and money was super neutral (i.e., it did not affect the economy due to any growth or change in rate).

The Phillips Curve

The Phillips curve is a major economic concept which many will come across while talking about inflation. Till date, many economists still believe that no work on inflation is complete without mentioning the Phillips curve. Therefore, it is important to know the link or connection between inflation and the Phillips curve.

Inflation and the Phillips Curve—What Is the Connection?

In November 1958, the economist A.W. Phillips wrote a paper titled 'The Relation between Unemployment and the Rate of Change of Money Wage Rates in the United Kingdom, 1861–1957',[9] which was published in *Economica*. Subsequent work extended this idea to inflation as measured by prices as well.

The Phillips curve states that there is an inverse relationship between inflation and unemployment. It explains that when inflation is relatively high, the unemployment rate is low, and when inflation is relatively low, the unemployment rate is high. But this also depends on the economic conditions of the time. That is, when inflation is relatively high and the economy is strong, unemployment is low, and when inflation is relatively low and the economy is weak, unemployment is high.

The validity of the Phillips curve was in question in the 1970s mainly due to stagflation. The trade-off between inflation and unemployment broke down during the 1970s. Stagflation mainly occurs when an economy's growth is stagnant, along with high inflation and high unemployment. This is the complete opposite of the Phillips curve. This led many economists to delve deeper into the subject of the relationship between unemployment and inflation. They found that the inverse relationship between inflation and unemployment could only hold in the short run, when there were no consumer or worker expectations. This is, thus, the link between inflation and the Phillips curve.

Empirical Studies on the Relationship Between Inflation and Growth Rate

There is a complex relationship between inflation and economic growth. There are empirical studies which have shown all kinds of relationships (positive, negative and neutral). The following are a few examples of the same.

Stanley Fischer (1993) stated that there was a negative relationship between inflation and growth rate. In his paper titled 'Role of Macroeconomic Factor in Growth', he did research on many macroeconomic variables, along with inflation, for 93 countries. He also found that inflation reduced economic growth by decreasing investment and productivity.

Robert J. Barro (1995) also came to the same conclusion by taking data from around 100 countries from 1960 to 1990, and examining the effects of inflation on economic growth or performance. He found that the impact of inflation on growth and investment was significantly negative.

Brian Motley (1994, 1998), in his paper titled 'Growth and Inflation: A Cross-Country Study', wrote: 'In almost all cases, inflation has a negative impact on real growth'. He further stated that '...inflation has a negative effect on real growth that is economically and in many cases statistically significant'.

Atish Ghosh and Steven Phillips (1998), in their IMF Staff

Papers research titled 'Warning: Inflation May Be Harmful to Your Growth', found and stated that: 'At very low inflation rates (around 2–3 per cent a year, or lower), inflation and growth are positively correlated. Otherwise, inflation and growth are negatively correlated, but the relationship is convex, so that the decline in growth associated with an increase from 10 per cent to 20 per cent inflation is much larger than that associated with moving from 40 per cent to 50 per cent inflation.'

Michael Bruno and William Easterly (1995) stated in their research paper that there was a negative relationship between inflation and growth. They stated that this negative relationship was firmly established even during a discrete high inflation crisis. They also stated that the growth effects of low to moderate inflation remained very vague. They concluded that inflation appeared to have a negative impact on growth.

In their research, Girijasankar Mallik and Anis Chowdhury (2011) found that there was a long-run positive relationship between inflation and the growth rate. They examined the relationship between inflation and GDP growth for four South Asian countries, namely Bangladesh, India, Pakistan and Sri Lanka.

Different Situations of Inflation and Economic Growth

There may be different situations where inflation can exist with respect to GDP growth. They are: i) **Situation 1**: more goods at the same price; ii) **Situation 2**: more goods at a higher price; iii) **Situation 3**: fewer goods at a higher price; iv) **Situation 4**: the same amount of goods at higher prices. Let us analyse these situations in brief, one by one.

Situation 1: More goods at the same price

When an economy's demand increases, the production of goods and services also increases to meet this demand. When production increases, unemployment decreases, and as a result, demand and wages also increase further. When wages increase, spending also increases. In this situation, there is inflation and an increase in the GDP.

Situation 2: More goods at a higher price

This is a more common phenomenon in any economy. When an economy's demand increases and there is a shortage of supply, prices are increased to meet the existing demand. To meet this demand, production has to increase, and therefore, more labourers or workers are hired. This results in a fall in unemployment, which leads to an increase in further demand and thus brings about an increase in prices. In this situation, the GDP and inflation both increase. This increase reaches an unsustainable level and then it becomes very difficult for policymakers to control inflation.

Situation 3: Fewer goods at a higher price

This situation is famously known as stagflation. In this situation, the GDP rises slowly, whereas inflation and unemployment increase due to the reduced production of goods and services.

Situation 4: The same amount of goods at higher prices

The economy produces the same amount of goods since there is no increase in demand from the consumers, but there is inflation. This is due to the reduced supply of raw materials or key commodities for production, and also inflation expectations. In this situation, both inflation and the GDP increase.

Other than these four, there is another situation—though it is not inflationary, it is still related to price levels—called a deflationary situation, where more goods are produced at lower prices. This results in deflation and diminished GDP growth. Among all these situations—including the deflationary situation—only one is unsustainable (situation 2), while the remaining three are helpful for economic growth. This clearly shows that the economy and inflation are well connected.

So What Is the Relationship between Inflation and Growth?

Now a question arises: what is the relationship between inflation and growth? Is there a direct relationship between economic growth and inflation? Well, finding the answer to this question is not easy, as we can see from the above theories.

Initially, they found that economic growth and inflation had a positive relationship. Then there are also views that there is a negative relationship between growth and inflation. There are also views which state that it is economic growth that reduces inflation, and not vice versa.

Henry Hazlitt, in his book *Man vs. The Welfare State*, stated: 'Inflation is not only unnecessary for economic growth. As long as it exists it is the enemy of economic growth. It distorts and falsifies economic calculation.'

This shows that there are also views where inflation is not necessary for economic growth. So there are many different views, from positive to negative, as well as ones which posit that there is no relationship between inflation and economic growth.

This is what was clearly stated by Milton Friedman in his book *Money and Economic Development*, where he put it crisply, 'So, historically, all possible combinations have occurred: inflation with and without development, no inflation with and without development.'

The IMF, in its Independent Evaluation Office report (2007), also stated that 'IMF policy staff acknowledge that the empirical literature on the inflation-growth relationship is inconclusive.'[10]

Therefore, it is quite evident that there is no conclusive theory or even empirical literature which can say that inflation and growth have any positive or negative relationship.

Inflation and Economic Growth—Walking on a Tightrope

Policymakers face a real challenge managing both economic growth and inflation. They go for contractionary policies when growth is at an above-average level, and for expansionary policies when economic growth is at a below-average level (as stated above, this varies from economy to economy). Economic policies need to be used to achieve both economic stability and price stability.

There are times when inflation and economic growth go in the same direction. This may be due to the following reasons:

1. The prices of certain goods or raw materials may increase, which may be completely unrelated to the business cycle. This relatively quick increase in the prices of specific goods may have an impact on overall inflation.
2. At times, past inflation can influence current inflation—despite the change in economic conditions. The economic slowdown may not have an immediate effect on inflation.
3. Inflation expectations play a vital role in determining inflation (we will examine this in detail in Chapter 9).

Policymakers cannot completely ignore the price shocks while formulating economic policies. Economic stability alone cannot provide price stability. When policymakers know the limits of economic stabilization, they can manage or sail through the business cycle (or cyclical fluctuations) without affecting price stability.

Inflation and economic growth are like walking on a tightrope which has to be handled with care. Inflation can make the economy grow and can also lead to depression. When inflation is too high, the economy suffers, and when inflation is too low, the economy suffers then as well.

However, if an economy can have inflation at reasonable levels—which purely and completely varies from economy to economy (i.e. country to country)—it may grow faster and become stronger. Policymakers need to ensure that their policy framework does not take care of just one economic variable (either the GDP or inflation), but both in order to have sustainable economic growth.

5

Inflation and the Stock Market

People invest in stocks for two opposite reasons—in hope and confidence in the future of an enterprise or in fear that the value of their capital will be lost through inflation.

—Bernard Baruch

The stock market is one of the indicators of how an economy functions. Therefore, it is necessary to understand its relationship with inflation, which is also one of the major indicators of the economy. It is also important to understand the effects of inflation on the stock market.

The Effects of Inflation on the Stock Market

The effects of inflation on the stock market may be positive or negative. These mainly depend on the investor's ability to hedge and the central bank's monetary policy decisions. The following are the main effects of inflation on the stock market:

1. The Purchasing Power of Investors

Inflation, by definition, is an increase in the general price levels of goods and services. As it has been seen in the previous chapters, it leads to a decrease in purchasing power or the value of money.

Therefore, inflation has a direct impact on the stock market. Investors are able to purchase only a few stocks for the same amount of money during inflation. When inflation rises in the economy, the present value of future cash flow goes down. When the value of money is reduced, the investors will be able to purchase a smaller quantity of stocks with the same amount of money compared to what they can buy today.

For example, if the existing rate of inflation is five per cent, then the receivable which was worth ₹20,000 before, is only worth ₹19,000 today.

When the purchasing power of investors gets affected, it tends to have a negative impact on the stock market.

2. Interest Rates and Valuations

The central bank of an economy increases its interest rates to curb or fight inflation. This increase in interest rates reduces the cash flow in the economy. The loans or the cost of capital increases, and as a result, the projected cash flows to companies come down. This results in a drop in their equity valuations.

An increase in interest rates also affects bond prices—as bond prices fall, it leads to a loss of capital for the investors.

3. Stocks

When there is high inflation, it leads to speculation about future stock prices. As a result of this, there is high volatility in the stock market. In the stock market, stocks are categorized into two groups: i) value stocks and ii) growth stocks.

1. **Value Stocks:** Value stocks are backed by strong cash flows. So these have a positive relationship with inflation—that is, these tend to move along with inflation. In other words, when inflation rises, value stocks also rise, and vice versa.
2. **Growth Stocks:** As growth stocks may have negligible cash flows, they have a negative impact on, or relationship with, inflation.

High inflation, or say rising inflation, hurts those stocks which generate income or pay dividends to the investors. As inflation increases, the dividends are not enough to cover it with the same amount of taxation. This results in a reduction in the dividends—as it acts as a double-edged sword, i.e., inflation erodes it from one side and taxation from the other.

4. Index

An increase in inflation affects the index of the stock market. When there is an increase in inflation, it impacts the economy in the form of less savings and spending. Due to less savings, the lending capacity of banks also comes down. This leaves the investors with a diminished availability of money to invest further, and as a result, the stock market index registers a negative impact.

There are empirical studies that have been carried out on whether inflation and the stock market have a direct or an indirect relationship (in other words, a positive or a negative relationship).

Empirical Studies on the Relationship Between Inflation and the Stock Market

It is a general notion that stock market returns always get affected whenever there is an increase in inflation. There are studies and findings which have established that there is a negative relationship between stock prices and inflation. At the same time, there are a few studies which point to a positive relationship between the two. Here are some of the empirical studies that have been carried out to highlight these relationships:

On 6 September 1929, Irving Fisher[11] was quoted in the *New York Herald Tribune* as stating: 'The present high levels of stock prices and corresponding low levels of dividend returns are due largely to two factors. One, the anticipation of large dividend returns in the immediate future; and two, reduction of risk to investors largely brought about through investment diversification made possible for the investor by investment trusts.' Fisher (1930), in his book titled *The Stock Market Crash and After*, stated that stock prices were positively related to expected inflation, providing a hedge against it.

James S. Ang and others (1979), in their research paper titled 'Evidence that the Common Stock Market Adjusts Fully for Expected Inflation', stated that a new empirical model based on theoretical analysis was developed and tested on Fisher's effect. The researcher confirmed the existence of Fisher's effect on the common stock market for the period between 1960 and 1975. They also concluded on Fisher's effect, saying that the common stock market fully adjusted itself on inflation expectations.

Martin Feldstein (1983), in his book titled *Inflation, Tax Rules and Capital Accumulation*, stated: 'The simple model developed in this paper conveys the idea of how a higher rate of inflation can cause a substantial reduction in the ratio of share prices to pretax earnings'. He found that there was an inverse relationship between higher inflation and lower share prices.

In 1985, René M. Stulz, in his working paper titled 'Asset Pricing and Expected Inflation', explained that the expected real returns on common stocks were negatively related to expected inflation and money growth. He explained his research with the equilibrium model and also stated that his research had pointed to a negative relationship between stock returns and unexpected inflation.

DO YOU KNOW?

After the Great Depression in the US, the stock market lost about 90 per cent of its value between 1929 and 1933. It took 25 years to recover.

In 1987, Gautam Kaul, in a research paper, investigated whether there was a negative relationship between stock returns and inflation. For explaining this relationship, he took up the equilibrium process in the monetary sector. He analysed data from four industrialized or developed countries (namely, Canada, Germany, the USA and the UK). From his data analysis, he concluded that there was a negative relationship between inflation and stock returns. He also went on to state that pro-cyclical movement in money, prices and stock returns in the 1930s revealed that there was a different relationship between stock and inflation. He said that stock returns either had a positive relationship, or no relationship with inflation variables.

Robert H. DeFina (1991), in his paper titled 'Does Inflation Depress the Stock Market?', found that unforeseen or unexpected inflation could substantially reduce equity values. In conclusion, he asked the title question, 'Does inflation depress the stock market?', and stated that it probably did, by discouraging business profits.

In 1998, Peter Sellin, in his research paper titled 'Monetary Policy and the Stock Market: Theory and Empirical Evidence', stated that empirical evidence showed that stock returns were adversely affected due to expected and unexpected inflation. He also stated that many empirical studies had explained this in numerous ways, and had proved that there was a negative relationship between inflation and stock returns. Therefore, it was no longer a puzzle.

John H. Boyd and others, in their 2000 research paper titled 'The Impact of Inflation on Financial Sector Performance', stated that they found that there was a significant and economically important negative relationship between inflation and financial development. They further said that sustained inflation and financial sector performance displayed a strong negative association.

In 2013, Chetan Yadav and others, in their research

paper titled 'The Study of Inflation and Stock Market Returns in Japan', examined the impact of inflation on stock returns in Japan for a period of ten years. They used a simple regression model to find the relationship between the dependent and independent variables. They stated that there was a positive, but not significant, relationship between stock market returns and inflation in Japan.

Evaluation of the Impact of Inflation on the Stock Market

When prices are rising, it is essential to understand and evaluate the impacts it can have on the stock market. This will help us understand the subject better.

1. Shares of Companies in the Growth Stage

Companies that are in the growth stage are expected to make more profits in the future, and are affected by inflation. As inflation reduces the value of money (or say, the profits), these companies (which are in their growth stage, or say, companies with growth shares) are impacted. Therefore, these companies should earn their income now rather than waiting for the future. This way, inflation would have a smaller impact on these companies as they would have a certain amount of hedge against it.

2. Moving from High-yielding Shares to Government Bonds

When there is high inflation, interest rates are also increased to curb or fight inflation. Shares with low growth and high returns or yield (for example, electricity utilities) are vulnerable to higher interest rates. When the interest rate increases, investors take out these kinds of shares and move them to government bonds and savings accounts. These would now earn comparably good returns, in contrast to high-returns or high-yielding shares.

3. Depends on the Type of Inflation

When there is strong economic growth, there is a gradual increase in price levels or, say, inflation. This inflation makes companies earn more profits. On the other hand, if there is stagflation, then the economy as well as individual companies are affected badly. Hyperinflation is another situation where the entirety of the savings may be wiped out due to inflation. During such times, the investment in buying shares of companies may offer a greater hedge against hyperinflation (the best example of this is the hyperinflation in Germany in the 1920s).

Risk Aversion and Inflation

Most investors tend to avoid taking risks and have a low tolerance for them. Investors prioritize their investments or their money over the possibility of a return on their money. They prefer liquid investments so that the money can be accessed whenever required, irrespective of market conditions.

Investors are always aware of this phenomenon—that inflation erodes earnings in the stock market. Therefore, to avoid risks, most of these investors generally invest in savings, government bonds, corporate bonds and certificates of deposits (CDs). In other words, they diversify their investment to hedge against inflation.

Inflation erodes savings faster than CDs and bonds. When the central bank increases interest rates to control inflation, the bond suffers. The bond's future cash flows get eroded due to inflation. Bonds are always better investments than stocks due to lower risks. Government bonds are better than corporate bonds as they are mostly exempted from taxes. This gives investors a hedge against inflation.

The Relationship between Equity Prices and Inflation

According to some theories, equities should offer a cushion against inflation. This is because inflation corresponds to an increase in nominal value, which boosts share prices. However, in practice, earnings vary from sector to sector, along with the ability of the producers to pass the higher costs on to the consumers so that their profit margins remain the same during inflation.

When inflation grows, the market frequently discounts these future cash flows with a higher interest rate. This means that equities are worth less in today's currency. Therefore, investors should naturally try to hedge their share earnings against inflation.

Is Inflation Always Bad for the Stock Market?

The answer to this question depends on so many other factors. If inflation is within the acceptable limit or tolerance level, where it indicates the growth of an economy, then it is not bad for the stock market. High inflation (i.e., inflation above the tolerance level) is always bad for the economy as a whole. Inflation that is within the tolerance level or the acceptable limit is good for the economy, as companies expect more demand and produce more. This, in return, earns more or makes a bigger profit, which increases the value of the stock of that company within the stock market.

6

Inflation and Fiscal Policy

Inflation is a form of tax, a tax that we all collectively must pay.

—Henry Hazlitt

Fiscal policy is a policy of the government whereby it adjusts its expenditure and tax rates. Inflation affects fiscal policies and vice versa. Monetary policies have a clearer mandate and better tools when it comes to handling inflation. The fiscal policy has more to do with the government's mandate, and most of the time its agenda is political. It is also important to understand how the fiscal outlook of the economy is affected due to inflation.

How Inflations Affect the Fiscal Outlook of the Economy

An increase in inflation affects the fiscal outlook of an economy in different ways—when other things remain constant or equal (ceteris paribus).

1. An increase in inflation will affect the primary deficit[12] in both ways, i.e. positive as well as negative ways. It mostly depends on government spending. With respect to government spending, the amount of spending goes up due to inflation—as the cost of goods and services also increases. In terms of tax revenues, the revenue also increases. This includes the tax on capital income as it tends to move along with inflation.
2. Government debt and government borrowings increase during inflation. When there is an increase in inflation, the cost of borrowing (or say, interest rates) increases. This affects not only new government borrowings, but also existing government debt as interest payments are increased. In simple terms, the fiscal deficit increases as it includes both government borrowings and interest payments.
3. When there is an increase in inflation, it is reflected in the nominal GDP.[13] When there is an increase in the growth of the nominal GDP, it is reflected in the fact that the fiscal outlook of the economy is doing better. The fiscal outlook of the economy helps the government go for more nominal borrowings or debt. This may increase the primary deficit as well as interest payments over time.

In the previous chapters, it was clearly explained that many economies are burdened with inflation because of financing their fiscal deficits over the years. Specifically, many economies' central banks went for printing money to finance their fiscal deficit, which played a major role in—actually created more havoc by—leading the economy towards hyperinflation.

Therefore, high inflation is always (and should be) a concern for every policymaker, as it can create havoc and disrupt the economy badly. Therefore, policymakers should handle inflation with the utmost care, as it can not only help the economy grow, but also destroy the economy if mishandled.

> ### DO YOU KNOW?
>
> The United States has experienced two currency collapses due to inflation. The first was the Continental currency during the Revolutionary War. The second was Confederate notes during the Civil War.

Can Fiscal Policy Fight Inflation?

This is one of the longest and strongest debates in the history of economics. Is it true that fiscal policy can help us fight or control inflation? Economists have different views on whether fiscal policy can do this.

The famous British economist John Maynard Keynes felt that fiscal policy could be used to combat inflation. When an economy is consuming more goods and services than it is capable of producing, then a reduction in government spending, as well as an increase in taxes, would reduce inflation, or say, inflationary pressures.

When there is an increase in taxes, consumers are left with less disposable income, which would make them curb their expenditure or spending. Thus, demand and supply would come to a state of equilibrium, which would reduce inflationary pressures or inflation. When there is a reduction in government spending, consumption also gets reduced indirectly through the multiplier effect, and thus, inflation is curbed. In this way, fiscal policy can help an economy fight or combat inflation.

How Fiscal Policy Can Help to Reduce Inflation

1. Fiscal Policy for Faster and Stronger Growth

As has been seen in the previous chapters, when inflation increases, interest rates are also increased to fight inflation. This discourages personal and business investment, and slows economic growth. There is also a risk of recession due to an increase in interest rates, as this may weaken labour markets and also threaten financial stability.

This is where the fiscal policy comes into play. When the fiscal policy addresses inflationary pressures, the monetary policy aims for the reduction of interest rates. A contractionary fiscal policy can reduce both demand and supply within the economy, whereas an expansionary fiscal policy can boost the supply side and cause economic growth.

The government, by reducing its deficit, also brings down long-term interest rates, which encourages private investors to invest more in the economy. In other words, there is a crowding-in effect (i.e., private investments are induced). This provides for faster and stronger economic growth.

2. Fiscal Policy and Budgetary Costs

When the government deploys a contractionary fiscal policy during inflation, the scale of interest rate hikes that is required also gets reduced. This reduces the net interest costs for the economy, which boosts both investment and growth. When the government decides to decrease the deficit, it is reflected in the reduction of the overall stock of debt. This lowers budgetary costs, along with interest payments (or say, fiscal deficit)—as the interest rate hike has already been taken care of.

3. Fiscal Policy Should Be in Tandem with Monetary Policy

To control inflation, economic policies (both fiscal and monetary) play a vital role. While using monetary policy tools, the central bank tries its level best to anchor inflation expectations. The government should reinforce the same in the economy through contractionary fiscal policies. By making fiscal adjustments, policymakers ensure that the government's economic policies are working in tandem to combat inflation. This reassures the economy and investors that both the fiscal and the monetary policy are working together to control inflation, and that they are taking it seriously. When the government tries to reduce its deficit during high inflation, it helps markets by reassuring them that it is committed to reducing or combating inflation.

4. Fiscal Policy Can Reduce Inflationary Pressures

The fiscal policy can boost the economy and reduce inflationary pressures. This is mostly carried out by encouraging the supply to meet the demand, rather than reducing demand to a state of equilibrium (i.e. supply = demand). When the fiscal policy is used to address inflationary pressures, it encourages investors to invest more and, thus, increase the supply to meet the existing demand. This reduces inflation.

5. Fiscal Policy to Combat Inflation within a Short Time Lag

The fiscal policy can be used to combat or control inflation, as it is effective in a short time lag compared to the tools of monetary policy. The macroeconomic effects of the monetary policy take months or even years to materialize and deliver the desired results. But the fiscal policy is a very effective tool as it delivers results with a very short time lag.

These were some major points detailing how the fiscal policy can help to reduce or combat inflation.

The Limitations of Fiscal Policy

There are no policy measures without limitations, and fiscal policy is not exempted from this. The limitations of fiscal policy are:

1. Political Agenda

The first limitation of the fiscal policy is that it is the government's mandate, which often has a political agenda or motive. Therefore, fiscal policy is not reliable.

2. Reduction of Government Expenditure

It is not easy to reduce government expenditure or spending, even during an inflation. This is because many developmental projects (including ongoing projects) have to be carried on and cannot be halted, as the costs will increase if inflation continues. Therefore, it is almost impossible to reduce government expenditure.

3. Impact of Increase in Taxes

An increase in taxes affects the economy badly, as this is a double-edged sword to fight inflation. When there is an increase in taxes, it affects savings and investments, which is reflected in the economy's output.

4. Flexibility

Since the fiscal policy is a mandate of the government and is guided by a political agenda, it is not flexible. Administrative issues need to be tackled with the utmost care, which requires a certain flexibility. This has an impact on the economy.

5. Decision-making and Implementation

Though the fiscal policy can be implemented in a short time, the decision-making process around fiscal-policy changes takes more time than the implementation period.

Is the Fiscal Policy a Panacea?

The answer is: **no.** The fiscal policy alone cannot tackle inflation. It is important for an economy that both the fiscal and the monetary policy should function smoothly, so that the economy can not only avoid a recession or depression, but also prevent overheating or hyperinflation.

The government should avoid more borrowings and

deficits to control inflation. This is because when the government's borrowings and deficit increase, the central bank opts for printing money to finance them. This increases the money supply in the economy (which is nothing but inflation).

7

Measures to Control Inflation

Inflation poses a serious threat to the growth momentum. Whatever be the cause, the fact remains that inflation is something which needs to be tackled with great urgency...

—Dr Manmohan Singh
Economist and former Prime Minister of India

Inflation is a serious problem—uncontrolled inflation adversely affects the economy. Therefore, it is important to control it. There are various measures to control inflation. These are classified into three categories: i) monetary measures, ii) fiscal measures, and iii) other measures.

Measures to Control Inflation

1. Monetary Measures

The central bank of an economy is responsible for controlling inflation through its monetary measures. There are various tools which the central bank uses to control inflation.

Rate of Interest: The central bank increases the rate of interest to control inflation. By increasing the rate of interest, the central bank curtails the money supply. When the interest rate increases, it discourages investors from investing and encourages people to save more. By doing so, the money supply in the economy is reduced.

> DO YOU KNOW?
>
> The post-Second World War hyperinflation in Hungary holds the record for being the most rapid monthly inflation ever: 41,900,000,000,000,000 per cent for July 1946, which means prices doubled every 13.5 hours.

Open Market Operation (OMO): OMO is one of the methods the central bank uses to control inflation and the money supply in the economy. When there is a surge in the money supply, the central bank uses this tool, i.e. OMO, to absorb excess money from the economy. The central bank issues government securities to commercial banks and others. Commercial banks spend money to buy these government securities, and by doing so, the central bank absorbs the excess money from the economy through OMO.

Cash Reserve Ratio (CRR): Raising the cash reserve ratios (CRR) is another monetary measure through which the central bank controls inflation. By raising the CRR, the central bank reduces credit creation. This makes commercial banks keep more cash deposited with the central banks as a reserve, and this reduces their lending capacity. This results in the reduction of the money supply in the economy.

Issuance of New Currency: Many may not be aware that the issuance of new currency is a monetary policy to control inflation. This is the most extreme monetary measure for tackling inflation. The central bank issues new currency in place of old currencies. One new note or unit of currency is exchanged for several old units of currency. This is a very effective measure during hyperinflation.

> ### DO YOU KNOW?
>
> A hyperinflation occurred in Germany in 1920, leading to great social unrest. The purchasing power of money fell so low that the German currency, the mark, became cheaper than firewood. Hitler blamed the Jews for the spiralling inflation, which helped pave the way for the Holocaust.

2. Fiscal Measures

Fiscal measures are measures taken by the government to control inflation. The main tools for fiscal measures implemented by governments are taxation and government expenditure. When the government decides to control inflation, it increases taxation, which in turn reduces the disposable income of the public and reduces the money supply. Along with taxation, the government also reduces its non-developmental expenditures to bring down inflation.

This can be explained with a chart. The chart given below depicts the movement of the aggregate demand (AD) from AD to AD1 due to fiscal measures. As price levels move from P to P1, the aggregate demand in the economy moves from AD to AD1.

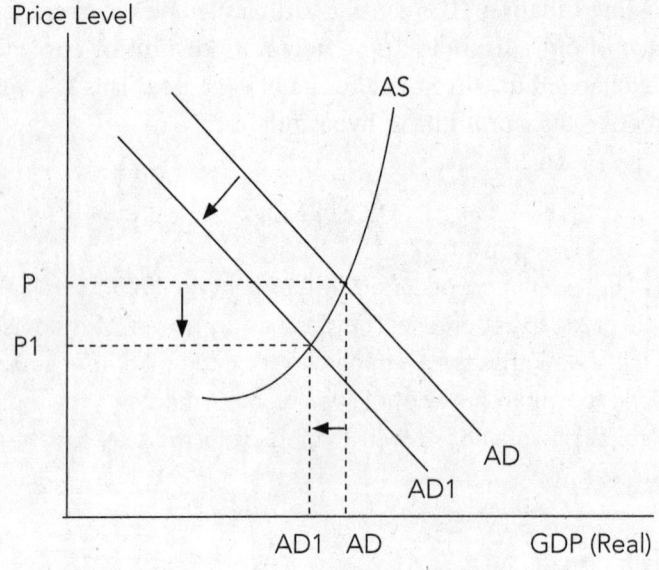

Chart 3: Effects of Fiscal Measures in Controlling Inflation

3. Other Measures

Price Control: This is another way to control inflation. The government fixes a ceiling limit for the prices of essential consumer goods, and selling them above these fixed prices becomes a punishable offence by law under this measure. However, in this method, inflation is suppressed (therefore, there is suppressed inflation) but it cannot be controlled for a long time. Historical evidence on price control shows that this measure only reduces the extent of inflation and cannot control it.

Rationing: Distributing scarce goods to a large number of consumers is called rationing. Mostly, essential consumer goods like rice, wheat, sugar and such others are rationed. It is a common belief that because of rationing, the prices of essential commodities stabilize within the economy.

Increase Production: Inflation is caused by an imbalance between the aggregate supply and the aggregate demand. Therefore, to control inflation it is essential to increase production, which will increase supply and bring about a balance (i.e. AS = AD).

Is There Any Cure for Inflation?

The cure for inflation is to stop the reasons behind it. In other words, remove the cause of inflation, which is an increase in the money supply (increased through money and credit). It sounds easy and simple, right? But it is not so.

From a fiscal policy perspective, with an increase in the budget deficit, it is not possible to control inflation. By itself, government expenditure is not a problem for inflation, but when the borrowing exceeds a certain limit, the government resorts to printing money to finance their deficits.

From a monetary policy perspective, the central bank should stop keeping its interest rates low for too long. In other words, it should stop its easy money policy to control more inflationary pressures. Remember, these things can have an impact on the overall economy. Therefore, the cure is neither easy nor simple.

Part B

India, Inflation and Monetary Phenomena

8

The History and the Present Scenario of Inflation in India

I do not think it is an exaggeration to say history is largely a history of inflation, usually inflations engineered by governments for the gain of governments.

—Friedrich August von Hayek

Inflation is an economic phenomenon which affects everyone in an economy. Inflation is just the rate of increase in prices. It is computed as a weighted average of the prices of individual goods and services. Using these weights, the general price index is constructed, which captures the overall range of prices of goods and services. Inflation is measured by index numbers. In India, it is measured in two ways. These are: i) consumer price inflation and ii) wholesale price inflation.

Basic Definitions

Consumer Price Inflation (CPI) (Base Year: 2012 = 100)

Consumer price inflation is inflation at retail prices, or at the consumer level. It is also called retail inflation as it collects prices which are quoted by retailers. The Central Statistics Office has classified CPI into three major groups: CPI Rural, CPI Urban and CPI Combined (also called CPI All India).

CPI Rural and CPI Urban reflect the change in price levels of various goods and services consumed by rural and urban populations, respectively. These indices are compiled both at the state (or union territory) level and the all-India level. The definitions of CPI Rural and Urban are as simple as the following: the CPI for the entire rural population is called CPI Rural, and the CPI for the entire urban population is termed CPI Urban.

Basket Composition

The basket composition of CPI Rural is constituted by 1,181 village markets covering all the districts in the country, with 268,351 quotations covering 225 items. CPI Urban is comprised of 1,114 markets covering 310 towns, with 281,001 quotations covering 250 items. CPI Combined (All-India) covers 299 items.

Table 3
CPI Rural and CPI Urban Basket Composition

Universe	CPI Rural	CPI Urban
Centres (Villages/Towns)	1,181 Village Markets	310 Towns (1,114 Markets)
Quotations	268,351	281,001
Items Covered	225	250

Other than this, there are CPI Agricultural Labourers and Rural Labourers (CPI-AL and CPI-RL), and CPI Industrial Workers (CPI-IW).

Agricultural Labour (AL) or Rural Labour (RL) (Base Year: 1986–87 = 100)

a) Agricultural Labour Households

Agricultural labour households are rural labour households which derive 50 per cent or more of their total income from wages paid for manual labour in agricultural activities.

b) Rural Labour Households

Households whose income in the last 365 days was derived more from wage-paid manual (agricultural and/or non-agricultural) labour, than from either paid non-manual employment or self-employment, are treated as rural labour households.

For both the indices, i.e. AL and RL, the all-India index is worked out as a weighted average of the indices of 20 states.

CPI Industrial Workers (CPI-IW) (Base Year: 2016 = 100)

The CPI numbers for industrial workers, a measure of change in the prices of a fixed basket of goods and services consumed by industrial workers over time, have been compiled and released on a monthly basis by the Labour Bureau since January 2006.

Earlier in the 2001 series, the index numbers were compiled for 78 industrially important centres selected across the country. A total of 88 centres were covered in the 2016 series, as opposed to the 78 centres in the 2001 series. The indices for all 78 centres were compiled at three levels, viz. sub-group, group and general.

The centre-specific index is compiled using weights derived from the Working Class Family Income and Expenditure Survey conducted during 1999–2000. In September 2020, the CPI-IW moved its base year from 2001 to 2016.

Wholesale Price Inflation (WPI) (Base Year: 2011–12 = 100)

The wholesale price inflation is the measure of price rise or inflation at the level of wholesale goods and services sold to retailers or small businesses. WPI baskets cover 697 items.

Other than this, policymakers use core inflation for their analysis as it removes the more volatile aspects of inflation (i.e., overall inflation minus inflation in the food and energy sectors).

In India, inflation has evolved over the years. It is important to understand how this evolution has taken place.

> **DO YOU KNOW?**
>
> Since Independence, the rupee has depreciated almost 20 times. In 1948, $1 was available at ₹4, and there was no debt in the country.

The Evolution of Inflation in India

Inflation in the 1950s: Under Control (1951–52 to 1959–60)

The decadal average rate of inflation in the 1950s was 1.7 per cent. The average inflation rate ranged from 12.5 per cent in 1952–53 to 13.8 per cent in 1956–57. The negative inflation rate in 1952–53 was due to bumper agricultural production, and the maximum inflation rate in 1956–57 was primarily credited to demand pressures (specifically to investment demand—both private and public) and measures for industrialization. In that decade (i.e. the 1950s) two more years witnessed negative price changes, 6.71 per cent in 1954–55 and 5.23 per cent in 1955–56. There was substantial volatility in the price movement during the 1950s.

Inflation in the 1960s: War and Famine (1960–61 to 1969–70)

During the 1960s, inflation accelerated. It was partly induced by two wars in 1962 and 1965. The average decadal inflation during the 1960s increased to 6.2 per cent. From 1968–69, inflation was 0.91 per cent. This was because of the bumper agricultural production in the previous year. Inflation was at its highest in 1966–67, as well as in the following year (i.e. 1967–68), and it was 13.95 per cent and 11.56 per cent, respectively. Inflation was at its highest in these two years due to the impact of the Pakistan War in 1965, and a famine during 1965–66. Inflation was higher in this decade compared to the previous one, but the differences decreased.

Inflation became a matter of serious concern as it breached the 20 per cent mark during the early 1970s, mainly due to inflation in international oil prices and the failure of agriculture production.

Inflation in the 1970s: Turbulent Period (1970–71 to 1979–80)

The most turbulent period for India in terms of inflationary uncertainty were the 1970s. In September 1974, India witnessed an extremely high rate of inflation when it reached 33.3 per cent. The very high inflation during the 1970s was primarily attributed to supply shocks from agriculture and oil prices.

The most awful inflation in India took place from November 1973 to December 1974, as it never dropped below 20 per cent and was above 30 per cent for four consecutive months from June 1974.

In its annual report, the Reserve Bank of India stated, 'It may be recalled that even the seasonal decline in prices, particularly agricultural commodity prices, to which the Indian economy is traditionally accustomed, did not take place during the last two years.' High inflation recurred in 1979–80. This was due to poor agricultural production and a hike in oil prices.

Overall, the 1970s was one of the highest inflationary decades for India, and this was due to heavy dependence on oil imports, and droughts or poor agricultural production.

Inflation in the 1980s: Troubles of an Expansionary Fiscal Policy and Monetization (1980–81 to 1989–90):

Inflation was high at 18.2 per cent in the beginning of the 1980s (in 1980–81). The inflation average of 7.2 per cent during the 1980s was an achievement, bringing about a reduction in inflation inconsistency. During the 1980s, there was a surge in demand pressure due to an expansionary fiscal policy and the printing of money (or monetization). This was accompanied by erratic supply shocks and it added inflationary pressure on the economy, though its severity was lower than that in the preceding decade.

India's fiscal deficit (i.e. the gap between revenue and expenditure) broadened from 3.8 per cent of its GDP in the 1970s, to 6.8 per cent in the 1980s. Nearly one-third of this fiscal deficit burden was borne by the RBI. The RBI expanded its credit to the government and this resulted in a speedy growth of reserve money, though the M3 was contained within 17 per cent (exactly at 16.9 per cent) with an increase in the cash reserve ratio. This excessive monetary expansion through the monetization of the fiscal deficit culminated in producing adverse effects on inflation. A vicious circle of high inflation, high deficits and high monetization was created by monetizing the fiscal deficit, which, in turn, led to a further increase in inflation.

The experience of the inflation-fiscal-monetary nexus was emphasized in the 1980s. Empirical evidence confirmed the harmful impact of excessive monetary expansion on inflation, resulting from the monetization of the fiscal deficit.[14]

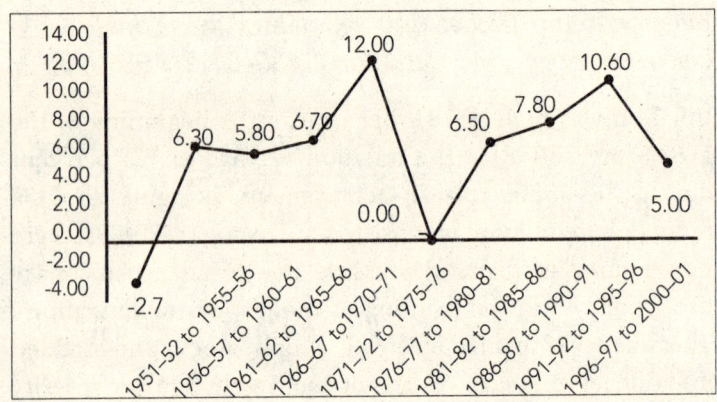

Chart 4: Inflation from 1952 to 2000–01

Table 4
WPI Inflation in India: Periodic Average

Period	Average Inflation (in %)	Range
1951–52 to 1955–56	-2.75	-12.78 to 6.51
1956–57 to 1960–61	6.3	3.03 to 13.79
1961–62 to 1965–66	5.8	0.0 to 11.1
1966–67 to 1970–71	6.7	-0.91 to 13.95
1971–72 to 1975–76	12.0	-1.1 to 25.2
1976–77 to 1980–81	8.5	0.0 to 18.2
1981–82 to 1985–86	6.5	4.4 to 9.3
1986–87 to 1990–91	7.8	5.8 to 10.3
1991–92 to 1995–96	10.6	8.1 to 13.7
1996–97 to 2000–01	5.0	3.3 to 7.2

Sources: (i) Economic Survey 2001–2
(ii) 'Indian Experience of Inflation: A Review of the Evolving Process', *Economic and Political Weekly*, January 2006

High inflation created a larger fiscal imbalance which necessitated greater monetization because government spending was more sensitive to inflation than government revenue. This led to a vicious cycle of high inflation, more fiscal deficits and massive monetization, which, in turn, caused inflation to rise even further.

Inflation in the 1990s: The Post-Reform Period

In 1991, an economic crisis occurred in India. This was primarily due to the balance-of-payments problem emanating from the high fiscal deficits and current account balances of the 1980s. In 1991–92, inflation was at 13.7 per cent. To solve the economic crisis, the government introduced many reforms in the industrial, external and financial sectors. These reforms increased foreign capital flows. The inflationary behaviour of the economy in the post-reform period can be divided into two sub-periods: i) in 1991–96, the average inflation was around 9.8 per cent, and ii) in 1996–2005, inflation came down to 4.9 per cent (which is half the rate witnessed in the first period).

Inflation was at a low rate of 3.3 per cent in 1999–2000, but it went up to 7.2 per cent in 2000–01. In 2002–03, the country faced a severe drought which made inflation stay at 3.4 per cent. Inflation eased from 6.5 per cent in 2004–05 to 4.3 per cent in 2005–06.

Overall, the decadal growth from 2000–01 to 2009–10 was around 5.4 per cent. The main reason for high inflation during this decade was the inflation of fuel prices, which was at around 8.9 per cent at this time. Out of this decade, the years 2000–01, 2003–04, 2004–05, 2006–07 and 2008–09 experienced higher inflation than the decadal average.

These years (except 2008–09) also witnessed high inflation in manufactured products due to the high prices of raw materials. The inflation in commodity prices and fuel prices was the main reason for high inflation in 2008–09.

The global slowdown, along with an unfavourable monsoon, had made for an abnormal year in 2009–10. The average inflation was at 3.6 per cent. This was supported by a negative inflation in fuel prices.

Present Scenario (2014 onwards)

In 2014, India moved from WPI as headline inflation to CPI as its goalpost. At present, the headline inflation is CPI Combined inflation. The yearly average inflation came down from 6.71 per cent in 2014 to 3.71 per cent in 2019. Inflation rose to 6.43 per cent again in 2020, during the pandemic. Yearly inflation came down to 5.14 per cent in 2021. The average yearly inflation in 2022 was 6.70 per cent, which declined to 5.66 per cent in 2023.

However, at present, though the average inflation has fallen to 4.95 per cent (as of December 2024), monthly inflation was at more than five per cent (exactly 5.22 per cent) in December 2024. The table and the graph given here show the movement of average inflation (year-wise):

Table 5
Yearly Average—Inflation Data from 2014

Year	CPI Combined—Inflation
2014	6.71
2015	4.91
2016	4.96
2017	3.33
2018	3.96
2019	3.71
2020	6.43
2021	5.14
2022	6.70
2023	5.66
2024	4.95

Source: CPI data from the CSO website, MoSPI; the yearly average was calculated from month-wise data given in Annexure II of this chapter.

India has witnessed a lot of fluctuations in its inflation rate for the past few decades. India is more sensitive to high inflation. In the post-pandemic period, India faced challenges posed by global demand-supply imbalances as well, like other economies in the world. However, it has done better compared to most of the other economies during the pandemic (i.e. Covid-19) as well as in the post-pandemic period, thanks to its conservative policymakers who always tried to control inflation. Despite ongoing geopolitical tensions, India is doing better than most other economies in the world, including advanced economies like the US, Germany and France. It had the lowest triennial average inflation from 2021 to 2023.

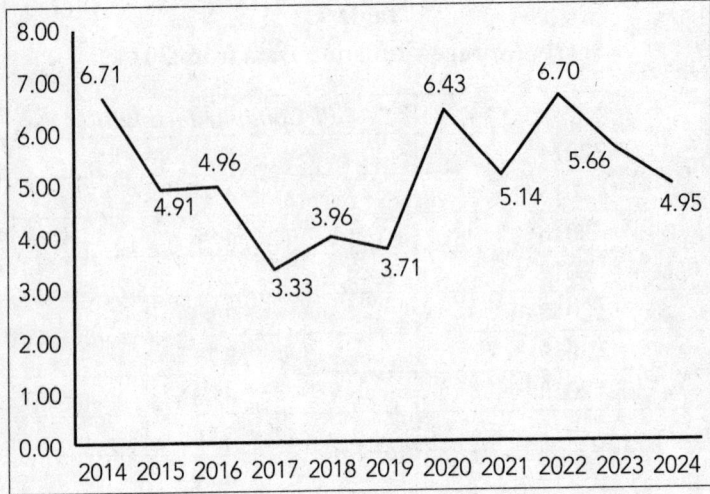

Chart 5: Calendar Year-wise Inflation from 2014
(See Annexures II, III and IV)

9

Inflation Expectations

I'm always a little dubious about an appeal to expectations as a causal factor; expectations are by definition a force that you intuitively feel must be ever present and very important but which somehow you are never allowed to observe directly.

—R.M. Solow (1979)

Inflation expectations can be simply defined as the expectations of consumers, producers/businesses and investors about the rate at which inflation is expected to rise in the future. Inflation expectations greatly influence actual inflation. That is why central banks' ability to achieve price stability depends on inflation expectations. Inflation expectations play a vital role in the effective implementation of the monetary policy. If a central bank can anchor the economic agents' inflation expectations close to its inflation objective, then its policy can achieve low and stable inflation.

What is meant by inflation expectations? How can we measure them? And how do policymakers use the information for forecasting, as well as controlling, inflation? These are normal questions when one thinks about inflation expectations. However, not all of these questions can be answered easily. In this chapter, an attempt is made to do the same.

The Definition of Inflation Expectations

The expected or anticipated value of the rate of inflation for some specified future period is known as inflation expectations. In other words, it is what people believe inflation could be in the future. It is the rate at which people or consumers, businesses and investors expect prices to rise in the future.

There are two kinds of expectations: forward-looking and backward-looking.

a) Forward-looking Expectations

These assume that people's expectations about the future are based on the structure of the economy and how the central bank responds to the information available to it at the time. It is also known as model-consistent.

b) Backward-looking Expectations

Expectations which are formed by looking at recent history or backwards are called backward-looking expectations. These are also known as extrapolative or adaptive expectations.

Key Variables of Inflation Expectations

Inflation expectations have three key variables. They are:

i) **Real Interest Rate:** The real interest rate is the difference between the nominal and expected inflation rates. This affects investments, consumption and savings.
ii) **The Fixing of Prices:** The prices which are fixed by firms incorporate the future prices of the factors of production. This includes capital and intermediate goods.
iii) **The Setting of Wages:** The setting of wages would keep the purchasing power of consumers and workers intact (even for future inflation).

Inflation expectations play a vital role in the proper formulation of the monetary policy. The success of the central bank's monetary policy depends on keeping these expectations close to its inflation objective.

The Importance of Inflation Expectations

1. Determining Actual Inflation

Inflation expectations play a vital role in determining inflation. According to economic theories, inflation expectations determine actual inflation. They also lead to changes in actual inflation.

2. Economic Policy Decisions

The success of the monetary policy to anchor inflation depends on inflation expectations. Inflation expectations play a vital role in economic decision-making.

3. Business Decision-making

For firms and businesses, the decision-making around inflation is important. The cost of future projects is based on inflation expectations. For example, higher inflation expectations may lead firms and businesses to increase their prices.

4. Improving Forecast Models

Inflation expectations can be very useful for improving forecast models. There are various models which are used for forecasting. All these models vary in their structure and complexity. The model which includes long-run inflation expectations performs much better than others.

The Advantages of Inflation Expectations

1. Inflation Targeting for Central Banks

Inflation expectations are very useful for the central bank of an economy to target inflation. They are used while making monetary policy frameworks to address inflation. Based on inflation expectations, an economy can adopt expansionary or contractionary monetary policies to target inflation.

2. Business Decision-making

A business makes decisions regarding its pricing, while negotiating wages, or on certain contracts on the basis of inflation expectations. They consider future investments, quantity as well as the pricing of their products based on inflation expectations.

3. Household Decision-making

Households can budget their consumption expenditure by factoring in inflation expectations. Households can also try to enhance their wealth avenues by saving or investing in the stock market to have a hedge against inflation.

Models and Theoretical Views on Inflation Expectations

1. The Keynesian Models

Modern macroeconomics was born in *The General Theory of Employment, Interest and Money* by John Maynard Keynes. His analysis came against the backdrop of the Great Depression. Keynes's General Theory never directly stated anything about the issue of inflation and it assumed that money wages were fixed. Only after the Second World War, which posed challenges for more government expenditure, did Keynes discuss the relationship between excess demand, wages and price inflation.

Inflation was becoming a greater concern for policymakers by the 1950s, and it was Alban William Housego 'Bill' Phillips who provided a path-breaking study on the relationship between unemployment and wage inflation. His theory went on to become the famous Phillips curve. It was in the 1960s that the Samuelson and Solow Phillips curve emerged. They interpreted a policy trade-off between reduced unemployment (or increased output) and lower inflation. They stated that if the government went for a reduction of unemployment, it would increase costs (inflation). They also pointed out that this trade-off between unemployment and inflation did not have to be stable. Thomas E. Hall and William R. Hart (2010)[15] stated, 'Samuelson and Solow never estimated their Phillips curve, but instead, hand drew it to fit the data for the twenty-five-year period from 1934 to 1958'.

In 1968, Milton Friedman stated that inflation expectations would disturb the trade-off between inflation and unemployment. In the short run, the Phillips curve would shift due to changes in inflation expectations. Regardless of the rate of inflation, output and unemployment would return to long-run equilibrium values. Keynesian economists took the concept of endogenous expectations and the natural rate of unemployment into the Phillips curve they estimated. It was found that policymakers could not run the economy without dealing with increasing inflationary pressure.

2. The Friedman-Phelps Phillips Curve Model

Friedman advanced his views in 1968. He argued that if inflation expectations were well anchored, then a stable relationship between inflation and unemployment could exist. He also warned that exploiting the short-run relationship between inflation and unemployment, as if it were a permanent phenomenon, would keep expectations unanchored. Then it would lead to a shift in the Phillips curve to the natural rate of unemployment. This called for a stimulative monetary policy which could lead to higher inflation without any increase in terms of unemployment in the long run.

Milton Friedman and Edmund Phelps independently challenged the theory of the Phillips curve. Both Friedman and Phelps believed that rational employers only paid attention to real wages. They further stated that real wages would adjust to the equilibrium point (i.e., the supply of labour would equal the demand for labour), and the unemployment rate would then stand distinctively linked with the rate of the real wage—the 'natural rate' of unemployment. The Phillips curve was negatively sloped in the short run, but in this framework, it shifted the vertical long-run Phillips curve upwards.

According to this expectations-augmented Phillips curve, inflation is dependent on both expected inflation as well as the difference between the actual and natural unemployment rates. In the long run, both unemployment and expected inflation are always equal to the natural rate of unemployment and actual inflation. When expectations are adjusted, the short-run Phillips curve also moves up to a point where it crosses the vertical long-term curve.

There is high inflation and no gains in terms of lower unemployment, which becomes the new equilibrium point. To keep the unemployment rate below the natural rate of unemployment, inflation needs to be accelerated. According to the expectations-augmented Phillips curve, the natural rate of unemployment is compatible with any rate of inflation, and the rate of inflation completely depends on the economic agent's expectations of future inflation in the long run.

There was a short-run trade-off between inflation and economic activity in the Friedman-Phelps formulation of the Phillips curve. Rational expectations were introduced by John F. Muth in his paper titled 'Rational Expectations and the Theory of Price Movements', published in 1961 in the journal *Econometrica*. However, rational expectations about the monetary policy were introduced into macroeconomic models by Robert Lucas Jr. in 1972.

As a result of this, Thomas J. Sargent and Neil Wallace (1975/76) concluded that the systematic monetary policy had no relevance in the short run. In the new classical approach, the anticipation of policy actions by forward-looking agents made the policy actions completely ineffective. In that case, only surprise or indiscriminate monetary policy changes would have an effect on the economy.

3. The New Keynesian Phillips Curve Model

According to this model, when real marginal costs increase, inflation also increases—as firms pass the higher costs on to consumers in the form of higher prices. When there are expectations of future inflation, firms increase their prices today, anticipating higher prices (or costs) tomorrow.

The economists Stanley Fischer (1977), John Brian Taylor (1980), Julio Jacobo Rotemberg (1982) and Guillermo A. Calvo (1982) revealed that the presence of staggered-contracts monetary policy might be effective even under rational expectations. Calvo developed a new pricing model which was the key building block of the New Keynesian models. This model combined sticky prices and forward-looking agents with monopolistic competition. It assumed that agents had full-information rational expectations (FIRE). It stated that even when there were distortions of market power and sticky prices, the monetary policy could improve and lead to an efficient allocation of resources.

A contemporary of Keynes's, Ralph George Hawtrey argued that the effectiveness of the monetary policy was determined by the expectations of a future policy stance as well as how agents took cues from current policy actions. Modern monetary economics supports the endogenous expectations viewpoint.

Jordi Gali and Mark Gertler (1999) stated that the New Keynesian Phillips curve defined inflation as a function of inflation and the output gap. The transmission mechanism of the monetary policy was affected by expectations. The monetary policy was affected by expectations through changes in asset prices and the time structure of interest rates.

Investments and consumption decisions depend on the long-term real interest rate. These long-term real interest rates are influenced by the future movements of short-term nominal interest rates and expectations of long-term inflation. There are wealth effects which depend on real returns, and this affects economic decisions. One of the problems with the standard New Keynesian Phillips curve model is that it does not fit data well.

According to Jeffrey C. Fuhrer (1997), inflation expectations are insignificant in explaining inflation using a purely forward-looking model. The hybrid New Keynesian Phillips curve states that inflation depends on both lagged and expected inflation.[16]

The transmission mechanism of the monetary policy is completely based on inflation expectations. If an economy's long-term inflation expectations are well anchored, then it can have a successful and effective monetary policy. The credibility of the central bank in achieving the objective of inflation control is completely dependent on the measures of inflation expectations.

Measures of Inflation Expectations

There are two measures of inflation expectations. These are survey-based measures and market-implied or market-based measures.

1. Survey-based Measures

As the name denotes, these measures of inflation expectations are based on surveys. These survey-based measures are classified into two categories: a) surveys of consumer expectations or consumer surveys, and b) surveys of professional forecasters' expectations. They both capture people's expectations in different ways, and are also constructed in different manners.

a) Surveys of Consumer Expectations or Consumer Surveys

As the name denotes, surveys taken from consumers are known as consumer surveys. But here, the survey is based on consumers' views on expectations about future inflation, and therefore, it is more specifically referred to as a survey of consumer expectations. These surveys differ from country to country, on the basis of their economic conditions and other factors. Some economies don't have any regular consumer surveys.

There are various factors which can affect the accuracy of the consumer survey measure of inflation expectations.

b) Surveys of Professional Forecasters

These are the forecasts made by professional economic forecasters, basically economists from the private sector who forecast their expectations about the inflation rate. These forecasts may vary from one year to 10 or 15 years in the future. These are considered as nearly or likely to be accurate, reflecting the true expectations that central bankers want to capture. These forecasts are updated less, compared to market-based measures.

2. Market-based or Market-implied Measures

This is the most common and the most frequently used measure of inflation expectations. It is measured as the difference between spot and forward rates on inflation-linked and nominal government bonds. These differences have four components: expected inflation, a liquidity premium, an inflation risk premium and other factors. Market-based measures are timely measures as they are available on a daily basis. From this measure, inflation expectations can be taken for the next 30 years. This measure reflects the decisions of financial market participants who are well informed and well resourced.

Inflation swap rates based on derivative instruments are another common market-based measure. These include not only inflation expectations, but also liquidity premiums and inflation risk premiums.

Both these methods help central bankers or policymakers develop a better understanding of how inflation expectations are formed and calculated at a different range of forecasts, apart from using surveys.

> ### DO YOU KNOW?
>
> Unlike the original Nobel Prizes (physics, chemistry, physiology, medicine, literature and peace), established by the Swedish industrialist Alfred Nobel at the end of the nineteenth century, the economics prize was instituted by the Swedish Central Bank (Sveriges Riksbank) in 1968, and is, thus, officially called the Sveriges Riksbank Prize in Economic Sciences in Memory of Alfred Nobel. Members of the Nobel family are known to have criticized the Swedish Central Bank for giving prizes to free market economists, of whom their ancestor would have disapproved.

Factors Determining Anchor Inflation Expectations

There are two major factors which determine anchor inflation expectations. These are:

1. Central Bank Transparency and Inflation Targeting

The central bank should be transparent about its monetary policy objectives. These objectives and rules should be very clear and well stated, and should be communicated with a clear objective. For many central banks across the world, inflation targeting is the primary objective.

Therefore, explicit or stated inflation targeting, along with transparency of rules and regulations of the central bank, can anchor inflation expectations. There is empirical evidence and studies which found that both explicit or stated inflation targeting, and transparency in the regulations, had anchored inflation much better.

2. Fiscal Policy

Fiscal policy is as important as monetary policy to anchor inflation expectations. The economy is unlikely to have well-anchored inflation without the help of its fiscal policy (especially fiscal sustainability). The public debt dynamics plays a major role in fiscal policy as it constrains the role of the monetary policy.

When interest rates are high in an economy, it implies that there is serious concern about that economy's fiscal sustainability (due to unstable public debt dynamics). There is empirical evidence and studies which found that the relationship between the public debt to GDP ratio and inflation volatility was positive, and they were significantly correlated.

Can Inflation Expectations Be Anchored?

There is mixed evidence on whether policymakers can anchor inflation expectations. There is some evidence which shows that firms update their decision on the basis of the relevant information provided by policymakers. Other evidence shows that it is extremely difficult to convey relevant information to firms.

Conventionally, the monetary policy anchors inflation by influencing nominal interest rates. However, real interest rates (i.e., nominal interest rate minus expected inflation rate) play a major role as they affect the economy directly. Real interest rates can make consumers either save or consume more, and also, they can alter the cost of borrowings for the investors to invest. Apart from this, there are other tools which the central bank uses to stimulate the economy, including non-conventional tools like quantitative easing, forward direction (i.e., communication about the future course of policy actions) and others. These tools are mainly used to keep nominal interest rates low, which has an impact on inflation expectations.

The information which policymakers provide to firms should be meaningful, so that firms and economic decision-makers make their decision more carefully. It is pertinent to say that policymakers should overcome information friction by ensuring whether the information was received by firms or economic decision-makers. There are studies which confirm that firms and economic decision-makers alter their decisions on the basis of new information they receive through the monetary policy.

Information Rigidity and Policymakers

The communication of new information from monetary policymakers (henceforth in this chapter, policymakers, until otherwise mentioned) to consumers and firms could influence economic behaviour. Yet, the question remains whether policymakers communicate new information to them. The present evidence on this issue is varied.

There is compelling evidence which shows that consumers and firms are ignoring or hardly giving any importance to information which could help them arrive at precise inflation expectations. Most firms don't give importance to aggregate inflation while making business decisions. Most firms are not even aware of monetary policies which can have an impact on inflation. There are firms which lack not only information but also knowledge about the objectives of the monetary policy and the central bank in the economy.

There is more evidence that policymakers overcome information friction exactly when decision-makers try to invest more resources to collect information about inflation. Depending upon the state of the economy, firms invest more or less to obtain new information about inflation. During critical times, policymakers try to communicate information to decision-makers to influence their inflation expectations.

There are also instances when the central bank's attempts to communicate information about policy objectives have affected consumers and firms. Therefore, policymakers as well as consumers and firms should try to enlighten each other by sharing information on inflation expectations. Policymakers should enlighten consumers and firms when there is critical information about inflation. This would help not only consumers and firms, but also policymakers themselves in anchoring inflation without much effort.

The Limitations of Inflation Expectations

Though inflation expectations can determine actual inflation, it is not without its limitations.

1. Divergence from Actual Inflation

Expected inflation often diverges from actual inflation. Expected inflation rarely becomes actual inflation. However, this is due to various other factors.

2. Time-consuming

The survey-based measure of inflation expectations is time-consuming. These surveys are undertaken by interviewing several households, which is certainly a time-consuming and laborious task.

3. Builds More Expectations

Mere inflation expectations can further build up inflation. The expectations of consumers, businesses, firms, workers and all economic participants may become actual inflation. Collective reactions to policy stances can increase inflation.

4. Affects Policy Decisions

Since the survey methods may not be accurate due to various reasons, they may not showcase the exact expectations of consumers and business firms. This affects the policy decisions made by policymakers on the basis of inflation expectations.

5. Affects the Economy

As policy decisions are affected by inflation expectations, the economy is also affected by these decisions. An inaccurate policy decision affects the economy as a whole.

Though there are limitations, there are also numerous advantages of inflation expectations. They enable decision-makers to make the right decisions in whatever role they play—in central banks, businesses and households. They serve as a safety measure while taking action and moving towards the desired goals. They also factor in the opinions and sentiments of various economic sections, which is very useful for making any decision. Though there are many studies and developing models which question whether inflation expectations have any impact on actual inflation, policymakers cannot ignore them as they play a major role in anchoring inflation. (*See Annexure V*)

10

Inflation Targeting

I have never believed that central banks should have rigid inflation targeting. That is not a good thing to stabilize. There is nothing in economic theory to back this.

—Robert Mundell

In the past decade, many central banks and monetary policymakers or central bankers have started to target the inflation rate directly to control the rise in the general price levels of goods and services. This new approach to dealing with an age-old problem through the monetary policy is called inflation targeting. The central bank of the country uses its monetary tools to move its actual inflation towards the targeted inflation rate or inflation target. Many economists favour inflation targeting and think it will lead to increased economic stability.

Why and How Does Inflation Targeting Work?

First and foremost, the question arises: why do countries choose inflation targeting? There are two specific reasons:

1. The central banks of these countries decided to achieve price stability through their monetary policy, which is a major contributor to economic growth.
2. Empirical evidence has shown that short-term manipulation of the monetary policy to achieve other economic goals, like higher employment and others, conflicts with price stability.

Inflation targeting helps to address this asymmetry by making inflation the primary goal or target of the monetary policy. It helps the central bank look ahead and tighten its policies before inflationary pressures reach their peak.

How Does It Work?

By adopting the technique of inflation targeting, the central bank forecasts the future path of inflation, along with the target inflation rate. The difference between target inflation and the forecast determines how to use monetary policy tools more effectively as well as which monetary policy tool to use. Countries that have adopted inflation targeting believe that they can improve the design and performance of the monetary policy with this practice, which the conventional procedures followed by central banks fail to do.

Are there any requirements for following inflation targeting? If so, what are they?

What Is Required for Following and Implementing Inflation Targeting?

For any economy to follow or implement inflation targeting, two important things are required. These are:

1. The monetary policy should have some degree of independence. It is a well-known fact that no central bank can be completely independent of the government. Yet, while they cannot be entirely independent, central banks should be free to choose their instruments to control the rate of inflation, and achieve what the government thinks is appropriate for the country.
2. The monetary authorities should not target any other economic indicators apart from inflation. They should not target economic indicators like employment, exchange rate, wages, and such others.

If these two basic conditions or requirements are fulfilled, then a country can conduct inflation targeting using its monetary policy. Other than these, the central bank authorities can take some basic steps, which are:

1. Set an explicit quantitative inflation target (rate) for a specific number of periods ahead.
2. State before the public clearly and explicitly that meeting the inflation target takes precedence over all other monetary policy objectives.
3. Develop an inflation forecasting model or methodology that employs a number of indicators containing information about future inflation.

4. Create a forward-looking operating procedure for adjusting monetary policy instruments (per forecasted inflation expectations) to achieve the desired target.

The Origin of Inflation Targeting and the Countries Which Have Adopted It

In December 1989, New Zealand became the first country in the world to adopt inflation targeting. Finland, Spain and the Slovak Republic are countries that took up inflation targeting but stopped after they adopted the euro as their domestic currency. Hungary, Poland, Armenia and the Czech Republic moved from being centrally planned economies to market economies. Once these economies transitioned, they adopted inflation targeting. After the 1997 crisis, which forced several countries to abandon fixed exchange rates, many emerging economies adopted inflation targeting.

DO YOU KNOW?

Italy, Greece and Portugal all published single-year targets for inflation at times during the early 1980s, and Sweden briefly operated a form of price-level targeting in the 1930s. However, none of these provided a complete or sustained structure for inflation targeting in liberalized markets of the sort now denoted by the term.

Source: Reserve Bank of New Zealand: Bulletin, Vol. 62, No. 3

In the 1990s, inflation targeting was adopted in New Zealand, Canada, the United Kingdom, Finland, Sweden, Australia and Spain (in chronological order of implementation or adoption).

The governments of New Zealand and Canada initially introduced targets to fight disinflation. The accomplishments of these two countries in taming comparatively high rates of inflation (in terms of industrial country standards) encouraged the other five countries to adopt similar policies, though their inflation rate was already comparatively low.

In the past 30 years, before adopting inflation targeting, these seven countries had a poor record of fighting inflation in comparison to Japan, Germany, the United States and Switzerland. It was generally perceived at that time (i.e., before these seven countries adopted inflation targeting) that they lacked monetary policy credibility.

Table 6
Inflation Targeting or Targeting Inflation across the World

Country	Inflation targeting adoption date	Target inflation rate at time of adoption	Country	Inflation targeting adoption date	Target inflation rate at time of adoption
New Zealand	1990	1–3	Philippines	2002	4 +/-1
Canada	1991	2 +/-1	Guatemala	2005	5 +/-1
United Kingdom	1992	2 (point target)	Indonesia	2005	5 +/-1

Australia	1993	2–3	Romania	2005	3 +/-1
Sweden	1993	2 (point target)	Republic of Serbia	2006	4–8
Czech Republic	1997	3 +/-1	Turkey	2006	5.5 +/-2
Israel	1997	2 +/-1	Armenia	2006	4.5 +/-1.5
Poland	1998	2.5 +/-1	Ghana	2007	8.5 +/-2
Brazil	1999	4.5 +/-2	Uruguay*	2007	3–7
Chile	1999	3 +/-1	Albania	2009	3 +/-1
Colombia	1999	2–4	Georgia	2009	3
South Africa	2000	3–6	Paraguay	2011	4.5
Thailand	2000	0.5–3	Uganda	2011	5
Hungary	2001	3 +/-1	Dominican Republic	2012	3–5
Mexico	2001	3 +/-1	Japan	2013	2
Iceland	2001	2.5 +/-1.5	Moldova	2013	3.5–6.5
Republic of Korea	2001	3 +/-1	India	2015	2–6
Norway	2001	2.5 +/-1	Kazakhstan	2015	4
Peru	2002	2 +/-1	Russia	2015	4

Sources: Hammond 2011; Roger 2010; and IMF staff calculations

Note: Countries are classified as inflation targeters based on the IMF's Annual Report on Exchange Arrangements and Exchange Restrictions (AREAER) database.

*For Uruguay, adoption date is aligned with the time when the interest rate became the main monetary policy instrument.

This table shows the dates of adoption of inflation targeting (or targeting inflation) across the world, irrespective of income levels.

> **DO YOU KNOW?**
>
> There is no single economic theory that can explain Singapore's economy. Almost all the land in Singapore is owned by the government, while 85 per cent of its housing is supplied by the government's housing corporation. Also, 22 per cent of its GDP is produced by state-owned enterprises (including Singapore Airlines), when the world average in that respect is only about nine per cent.
>
> To put it bluntly, there isn't one economic theory that can single-handedly explain Singapore's success; its economy combines extreme features of capitalism and socialism. All theories are partial; reality is complex.

Empirical evidence shows that inflation targeting is very helpful in anchoring inflation expectations, bringing inflation under control or lowering it, and reducing the volatility of inflation. Moreover, all these targets are achieved without any adverse effect on interest volatility and the output of the economy.

In 2018, some studies found that inflation targeting was very effective even in emerging market economies. In some countries, the adoption of inflation targeting was complemented by better fiscal disciplines (especially in Latin America). By adopting inflation targeting, some emerging economies took steps to strengthen and develop their financial sector. This shows that the adoption of inflation targeting as a monetary policy measure is very effective, not only for policymaking but also for securing wider economic benefits.

According to Charles Freedman and Douglas Laxton (2009), there are six principles of inflation targeting. These are as follows:

1. **Nominal Anchor:** The primary role of monetary policy is to provide a nominal anchor for the economy, and giving weight to other objectives must not be inconsistent with providing an anchor for inflation and inflation expectations.
2. **Effective Inflation Targeting:** Reducing uncertainty, stabilizing inflation expectations, and lowering the frequency and severity of boom-bust cycles are some of the positive first-order welfare benefits of effective inflation targeting.
3. **Other Government Policies:** The effectiveness of an inflation-targeting regime depends on other government policies that make the case for monetary policy easier and more reliable.
4. **Inflation Forecast Targeting:** Due to lags in the monetary transmission mechanism and concerns about the deviation of output from its potential and of inflation from its target, it is neither feasible nor desirable to maintain inflation exactly on target. So in practice, inflation targeting is replaced by inflation forecast targeting.
5. **Independence from Political Processes:** In order to fulfil their goals, central bankers need to be sufficiently independent of political processes and have goals

that are adequately defined in comparison to other objectives.

6. **The Need for Effective Monitoring:** Effective monitoring and accountability mechanisms are required to ensure that central bankers act in a manner consistent with stated goals and sound practices.

There is always a time lag between the central bank's policy and its impact on inflation in the economy. It is pertinent to understand that inflation targeting focuses on the expected future rate of inflation and not the present rate thereof. Present policy measures will not affect the present inflation rate as it is a result of past policies and economic shocks.

When the central bank debates inflation targeting, the focus is on the expected inflation rate over the policy period—the timeframe within which the central bank expects inflation to return to its target—following economic shocks and policy actions.

No policy work or theory is without limitations. Inflation targeting also has those.

Limitations of Inflation Targeting

1. Too Much Focus on Inflation or Ignoring Other Goals

Inflation targeting makes policymakers (central bankers) focus too much on inflation and ignore other economic objectives. By opting for more focus on inflation control, policymakers may ignore other economic problems or issues like unemployment and growth. Also, inflation targeting cannot remove supply bottlenecks, or supply chain problems.

2. Flexibility

Since the mandate of the monetary policy is very clear about inflation targeting being its main objective, there is hardly any scope for flexibility. This may be a hurdle for fiscal measures to stimulate the economy.

3. Financial Stability and Financial Inclusion

The primary function of any central bank should be ensuring financial stability. When an economy opts for inflation targeting, it has to address financial stability and inclusion. However, policymakers often ignore this and hardly provide any support when there is an issue in the financial system.

4. Exchange Rate Volatility

Inflation targeting often paves the way for speculative behaviour. This may give more space to external shocks and volatility in the exchange rate. Inflation targeting cannot stabilize this volatility in the short run.

5. Policy Coordination

For any economy, policy coordination is very important to achieve the desired goals. In many economies, there are no properly coordinated fiscal or monetary policies. Therefore, it is important to have clarity about the desired goal for both policies before implementation. This requires proper coordination and communication between both channels of policymakers.

Is Inflation Targeting a Panacea?

No, it is definitely not a panacea. When it comes to policymaking, there can be no single policy tool or mechanism which can make the economy better or more stable. Inflation targeting has been adopted by many countries over the past 30 years (since its adoption in New Zealand). The effectiveness of inflation targeting depends on the economy which implements it—a country should assess its economy before adopting it, and it should also make changes according to its economy's needs. (*See Annexure VI*)

11

Monetary Policy and Inflation Targeting in India

Inflation is as violent as a mugger, as frightening as an armed robber and as deadly as a hit man.

—Ronald Reagan

On 1 April 1935, the Reserve Bank of India (RBI) was formed as a shareholders' institution. In 1949, the RBI was nationalized and came to be owned by the government of India. According to the preamble of the RBI Act of 1934, the objective of the RBI is:

> ...to regulate the issue of Bank notes and keeping of reserves with a view to securing monetary stability in India and generally to operate the currency and credit system of the country to its advantage; to have a modern monetary policy framework to meet the challenge of an increasingly complex economy, to maintain price stability while keeping in mind the objective of growth.[17]

The main functions of the RBI are: a) issuing currency, (b) being a bankers' bank (or banker to other banks), and c) being a banker to the government.

The Evolution of Monetary Policy in India

Formative Years or Early Phase (till 1951)

In the initial years of the RBI, there was no formal monetary policy formulation. It was only administering the demand and supply of credit. It had three tools—the bank rate, the reserve requirement, and open market operations (OMO). The bank rate is the rate at which the RBI is willing to buy or discount bills of exchange (including other commercial paper eligible for purchase under Section 49 of the RBI Act). Open market operations refer to buying and selling securities to scheduled commercial banks, and the reserve requirement is a proportion amount of total deposits which has to be kept with the central bank or the RBI. These are the three basic tools which the RBI uses for credit availability.

The bank rate was hardly used during the formative years. It was used only once in November 1935 (the rate was reduced from 3.5 to 3 per cent) and kept unchanged till 1951. However, the OMOs were substantially used by the RBI during this period.

The Development Phase

India launched its first Five-Year Plan in 1950. The role of the monetary policy was aligned with this crucial development and planning process. The role of the monetary and credit policy was emphasized in the First Five-Year Plan. This phase is considered the developmental phase (1951 to 1990) of the role of the central bank.

The RBI was asked to put in place an appropriate institutional framework for developmental needs by mobilizing savings and promoting financial intermediaries and investments. In 1956, after the adoption of the Indian Constitution (1950), the States Reorganisation Act was enacted. This expanded the RBI's role as a banker to the government, so it had to facilitate the integration of currency and banking operations in India.

This also provided the RBI the ability to exercise control over all the banks in India. Accordingly, the Banking Laws (Amendment) Bill, 1967, was introduced, and this was followed by the nationalization of 14 private commercial banks in 1969.

During this phase, the introduction of a formal monetary policy came into effect. The need for a monetary policy emerged out of the necessity to balance financial stability and developmental functions. In this phase, inflation was mostly controlled by selective credit controls and moral suasion by the RBI to restrain banks from extending credit for speculative purposes. On the fiscal side, the government used price controls.

The Monetary Targeting Phase

In 1973, the Bretton Woods Agreement collapsed, and this led to a paradigm shift in the global economy from a Keynesian to a monetarist approach. Most developed countries began to focus on either their monetary reserves or inflation targeting.

From the 1970s till the mid-1980s, the RBI was financing the large deficits of the government. This resulted in a significant increase in the money supply (inflation). India also began to rethink its stand on monetary policy. At this juncture, the RBI set up a committee under the chairmanship of Dr Sukhamoy Chakraborty in 1985 to review the working of the monetary system. The committee suggested that the monetary authority should target money in a more formal and secure way. It advised it to target broad money (M3) supply with feedback. Accordingly, by the mid-1980s, the RBI evolved its new formal framework of monetary policy, targeting broad money supply as a nominal anchor.

The statutory liquidity ratio (SLR) and the cash reserve ratio increased gradually in the 1980s to reach their peak by the early 1990s. After this, as a precautionary measure, the SLR and CRR were reduced to meet the capital requirements of the economy.

The Multiple Indicators Approach (MIA)

In 1991, India went for liberalization and globalization. This added completely new and different dimensions to the responsibilities of the RBI, from financial reforms to aligning the monetary policy framework with global trends, along with a domestically suitable framework for India. From the mid-1980s, India followed a flexible monetary target approach until 1998.

Since 1999, India has moved from a flexible monetary target approach to the new monetary policy framework, known as the multiple indicator approach (MIA). This approach includes multiple variables like money, credit, output, trade and capital flows, fiscal indicators or situations, inflation rate, exchange rates and interest rates. Dr Bimal Jalan, the then RBI governor, had conceptualized this approach. This was implemented in two stages, the first with economic and financial variables, and later, forward-looking variables and time series models were added to it.

In the MIA framework, the policy emphasis was shifted from the quantity of credit to the interest rate (or price of credit). Short-term interest rates were the key instruments of the RBI's monetary policy stance. With this policy stance, the RBI brought its liquidity operations to align with market rates. Till 2016, India followed the multiple indicators approach. The MIA was successful in keeping inflation low and growth high until the global financial crisis.

The credibility of the MIA framework came into question after the global financial crisis in 2009, and especially after the 'taper tantrum' episode in 2013. These two episodes raised the question of whether it was possible to have low growth and persistently high inflation at the same time. As the MIA did not provide a clearly defined anchor for the monetary policy, an expert committee was set up for this purpose by the RBI.

Shifting towards Flexible Inflation Targeting

The expert committee was set up to revise and strengthen the monetary policy framework under the chairmanship of Dr Urjit Patel. The committee submitted its report in January 2014. It recommended inflation as the new anchor for the monetary policy. It defined inflation as headline consumer price index (CPI) inflation—CPI Combined. In June 2016, India formally adopted flexible inflation targeting with the amendment of the RBI Act. The act now stated:

'the primary objective of monetary policy is to maintain price stability while keeping in mind the objective of growth'. Thus, India entered the new monetary policy framework of flexible inflation targeting.

Flexible Inflation Targeting

On 5 August 2016, under Section 45ZA, the government of India, in consultation with the Reserve Bank of India (RBI), notified the inflation target in the Gazette of India. In that gazette notification, it was announced that the consumer price index would be the inflation target, and the target period would be five years from the date of announcement (i.e., from 5 August 2016 to 31 March 2021). On 31 March 2021, the central government retained the inflation target as well as the tolerance level for the next five-year period (i.e., 1 April 2021 to 31 March 2026). The inflation targets,[18] along with the upper and lower tolerance limits, were as follows:

Inflation Target	Four per cent (4%)
Upper Tolerance Level	Six per cent (6%)
Lower Tolerance Level	Two per cent (2%)

Inflation targets are determined by the government in consultation with the Reserve Bank of India once in five years. The consumer price index is the goalpost for inflation targeting. Once the inflation target is determined, the government notifies it in the official gazette. The Reserve Bank of India organizes at least four meetings of the Monetary Policy Committee (MPC) a year, and also publishes its schedule in advance.

Every six months, the RBI is asked to publish a monetary policy report along with an explanation of the sources of inflation. The report is supposed to contain: i) the resolution adopted by the committee, ii) the minutes of the proceedings of the meeting, iii) the vote, iv) the statement of each member of the MPC, and v) a document explaining steps to be taken to implement the decisions of the MPC. On the fourteenth day after every meeting of the MPC, the RBI is supposed to publish forecasts of inflation for the period of six to 18 months.

Finally, if the RBI fails to meet the inflation target, it is supposed to submit a report explaining the reasons for its failure to achieve it, and suggest remedial actions, along with an estimated time period within which the inflation target can be achieved.

The success of inflation targeting is mainly dependent on the transmission mechanism.

Transmission Mechanism in Monetary Policy

Conventionally, there are four channels of the transmission mechanism in the monetary policy. These are: interest rates, credit aggregates, asset prices and exchange rate channels. In India, the transmission mechanism takes place normally through price-based instruments (LAF) and quantity-based instruments (CRR and SLR). Other than these, there are exchange market channels and expectations.

1. Liquidity Adjustment Facility (LAF)

The reformed monetary policy framework was crystallized into a liquidity adjustment facility (LAF) and introduced in three phases starting in 2000. The LAF was amended on 3 May 2001.

Under the LAF, the RBI sets its policy rates, namely the repo rate and the reverse repo rate. These provide a corridor for overnight money market rates. The LAF policy rates are also known as price-based instruments as they directly affect the system and are mainly targeted towards anchoring inflation. The RBI uses these instruments to bring down inflation within the target range [i.e., the inflation targets of +/-4 (+/-2)].

Repo stands for the repurchase option. Commercial banks borrow money from the RBI by selling their securities, with an agreement to purchase the same at fixed (mostly higher) prices on a specified future date. The RBI charges an interest on these transactions and its rate is called the repo rate. In other words, the difference between the selling prices and the purchasing prices of these securities is called the repo rate. An increase in the repo rate absorbs (reduces) liquidity from the system or the economy, while a decrease in the repo rate injects more liquidity into it.

As the name denotes, the reverse repo rate is the opposite of the repo rate. When the RBI decides to borrow money from commercial banks by lending securities, it absorbs liquidity from the system. The interest rate at which the RBI borrows money from the commercial bank is called the reverse repo rate.

2. Bank Credit and Lending Rates—CRR and SLR

A portion of deposits from commercial banks needs to be kept with the RBI in the form of reserves. This is called the cash reserve ratio (CRR). When the RBI increases the CRR, it reduces loanable funds with the commercial banks, and thus absorbs liquidity from the system. When the RBI reduces the CRR, loanable funds with commercial banks increase, and this injects liquidity into the system with bank credits.

Every commercial bank needs to retain a certain percentage of liquid assets of their net time and demand liabilities (NDTL). This reserve can be maintained in the form of cash, securities and gold. Mostly, it is held in the form of government securities. This reserve is evaluated as a percentage of the value of the bank's liquidity, divided by the whole of its NDTL. This ratio of liquidity to NDTL is known as the statutory liquidity ratio (SLR). An increase in SLR diminishes loanable funds for the banks, and thus reduces liquidity in the system. A decrease in SLR increases loanable funds, and thus injects liquidity into the system. These two are also known as quantity-based instruments.

3. Exchange Rate Market Channels

An increase in policy rates leads to the strengthening of the domestic currency. Due to the increase in interest rates, Indian assets get more attractive and there is greater capital flow in the economy. This strengthens the exchange rate of the rupee.

When there is an appreciation of the currency in the exchange rate market, it impacts the economy in two major ways:

1. There is an increase in imports and a decline in exports. This is because foreign goods become cheaper compared to domestically produced goods.
2. This has an impact on inflation. As the rupee strengthens, imports can be made at a lower price. Since imported goods and import-substitute goods become cheaper, inflation is tamed.

Though exports are reduced and imports become cheaper through this channel, and inflation is tamed, the GDP of the economy also shrinks.

4. Expectations

With increasing integration and the growing openness of the Indian economy with the rest of the world, geo-economic (global economic factors) and financial developments are also shaping expectations. The RBI also takes such factors and expectations into consideration while formulating a monetary policy framework. Over the years, inflation expectations have assumed importance while conducting the monetary policy.

Inflation expectations due to geo-economic factors are considered while taking monetary policy decisions. When policymakers communicate clearly, their standpoint on the economy and whether further hikes are going to happen or not provides the public the assurance that policymakers are serious about inflation.

Other than these four important channels of transmission mechanism, there are the debt market channels and the assets price channels.

Inflation Targeting during the Pandemic and in the Post-Pandemic (Covid-19) Period

During the pandemic, many global economies faced demand-supply imbalances. India was no exception to this. Due to these imbalances, many economies around the world (including advanced ones) experienced high inflation. However, India fared better in terms of inflation than many advanced economies in the world. The average inflation rate in India was within the range of two to six per cent in 2024. The triennial average from 2021 to 2024 had the lowest deviation from the inflation target compared to many economies in the world.

Despite global tensions due to ongoing wars, India has managed to keep its inflation within the target, and has witnessed less deviation from it even during the pandemic and in the post-pandemic period. This is due to India's conservative policymakers who have always taken appropriate actions to control inflation. Therefore, India has not experienced higher inflation (though we may feel that the present rate of inflation is higher), unlike other economies in the world.

Empirical studies show that after adopting the inflation target regime, India's inflation expectations are better anchored, inflation is stable and lower, and there is a better transmission mechanism of the monetary policy.

There are no policy frameworks which are without any challenges, and inflation targeting is definitely beset with challenges.

Challenges for Implementing Inflation Targeting (or Flexible Inflation Targeting) in India

Transmission Mechanism

For any economy, the transmission mechanism of the monetary policy is the biggest challenge. India is no exception to this. It is important to find the crucial aspects of the monetary policy transmission mechanism that are unique to India. Though there are multiple channels for the transmission mechanism, the interest rate is the most important one. If this transmission channel functions efficiently, then the monetary policy will be effective, and vice versa.

Food Prices in the CPI

In India, about 46 per cent of the CPI basket is constituted by a food group—the huge proportion of food in the CPI poses an important challenge for the implementation of inflation targeting. Indian food prices are quite vulnerable to supply shocks—this often manifests in the form of unpredictable rainfall and its impact on agricultural production. Other than this, the government intervenes in agricultural production and the sale of agricultural products by taking steps such as setting minimum support prices, employment guarantees and minimum wages.

A well-established inflation targeting system offers an effective strategy to address supply-shock effects. This is done in two ways—first, the RBI should provide a credible long-term inflation target to anchor inflation expectations. Second, the RBI can reinforce the anchor by publishing the forecast which shows the medium-term path back to the target.

By doing so, the inflation-targeting system gains more credibility and wins the confidence of the public.

Credibility

Credibility can be earned over time by achieving the announced objectives, and by efficient and clear communication. Credibility is lost if policy actions are inconsistent with the announced objective. Even if the central bank raises the policy rate, the effect on the economy, especially during inflationary shocks, depends on public perception of the action announced by the RBI.

These three are the major challenges for the implementation of inflation targeting in India. Other than these, there is fiscal dominance which can affect the efforts of the RBI if the objectives of government policies and the RBI are not along the same lines. (*See Annexures VII and VIII*)

12

Is Inflation Always and Everywhere a Monetary Phenomenon, and Is It Applicable to India?

Continued inflation inevitably leads to catastrophe.

—Ludwig von Mises

Before dwelling on Milton Friedman's famous statement about inflation being a monetary phenomenon, and discussing whether it is true or not and whether it is applicable to India, it is important to understand the limitations of monetary policies.

Limitations of Monetary Policy

The following are the general limitations of monetary policy in controlling inflation, and these are not limited to India:

1. Imperfect Money and Credit Markets

The monetary policy may not be effective in controlling inflation when an economy has imperfect money and credit markets. When an economy's money and the credit market is not well developed, the monetary policy is not going to be effective. This is because there would not be a smooth transmission mechanism in the economy, and eventually there would be policy failure.

2. Time Lag

The implementation of the monetary policy takes a long time to deliver results. This reduces the effectiveness of the monetary policy to control inflation. Until the results of previous policy implementations are visible, a further policy framework cannot (should not) be carried out blindfolded.

3. Inflation Does Not Occur Only because of Monetary Aggregates

The monetary policy can control inflation only to a certain extent. This is because inflation may occur not only due to monetary aggregates like credit creation and money supply, but also due to other factors like supply bottlenecks.

4. Expectations

The monetary policy becomes completely ineffective if investors and producers expect to earn more profits because the economic fundamentals of the economy are strong and the future conditions of the economy are going to be better. The mere expectation of a bright future can nullify the effectiveness of the monetary policy.

5. Inability to Remove Supply Chain Problems

The monetary policy can control inflation only to a certain extent because it cannot remove supply chain problems in the economy. If the economy is facing supply chain problems, the monetary policy becomes ineffective as it cannot boost the supply.

These limitations also show us that inflation may not always and everywhere be a monetary phenomenon. Now, it is important to understand what Milton Friedman said before getting into the question of whether inflation is always and everywhere a monetary phenomenon, and whether it applies to India.

Monetary Phenomena and the Quantity Theory of Money

Milton Friedman's famous statement is based on the quantity theory of money which demonstrates the relationship between money supply and prices. Irving Fisher's equation of exchange was **MV = PT**, but these days it is written as:

$$MV = PQ$$

In the equation, **M** stands for money supply, **V** stands for velocity of circulation of money, **P** stands for the average or aggregate price level, and **Q** stands for real output (whereas in the original equation, T stood for the total number of transactions).

The equation is the symbolic representation of the relationship between money and inflation. It implies that inflation increases when the money supply exceeds economic activity and when the velocity of money is constant.

Milton Friedman's Monetary Phenomenon

In *The Role of Monetary Policy*, Milton Friedman stated:

> The first and most important lesson that history teaches about what monetary policy can do—and it is a lesson of the most profound importance—is that monetary policy can prevent money itself from being a major source of economic disturbance [...] There is, therefore, a positive and important task for the monetary authority—to suggest improvements in the [monetary] machine that will reduce the chances that it will get out of order and to use its own powers so as to keep the machine in good working order...
>
> A second thing monetary policy can do is [to] provide a stable background for the economy [...] Our economic system will work best when producers and consumers, employers and employees, can proceed with full confidence that the average level of prices will behave in a known way in the future—preferably that it will be highly stable.

From the above statements, it is clear that Friedman used the term 'monetary policy' in a very broad context, compared to how it is defined today. Friedman emphasized that the primary role of the monetary policy was to facilitate the smooth functioning of the financial system, and controlling inflation was only a secondary function. Friedman laid stress on the task of maintaining financial stability in a crisis. During a crisis, the way a central bank acts as a lender of last resort has an impact on price movements.

Friedman, in his *American Economic Review* address, stated that there was no trade-off between price stability and full employment or 'maximum employment' in the language of the Federal Reserve Act, if interest rate policy was carried out to achieve low and stable inflation.

Theoretically, there are two views on how the inflation rate is determined: i) monetary dominance or ii) fiscal dominance. The former is a view that the government formulates a fiscal policy which is consistent with the central bank's pursued goal. This is normally a perceived path of the monetary policy that determines inflation. However, if the government does not implement fiscal reforms, especially when finances are deteriorating, then the central bank is forced to choose between two evils: inflation or financial system instability. In this case, the price path is determined by the perceived fiscal path and the central bank's reaction to it.

In today's world, how the central bank can avoid fiscal dominance is a greater issue. Unfortunately, Friedman's proposition does not address such challenges or the problems which central bankers face in the real world. In such situations, it is important how central banks perceive and support the logic behind their monetary policy implementation.

What about an open economy? How does Friedman's proposition work there? Empirical evidence suggests that every policy decision taken from the perspective of the individual economy has a spill-over effect. Therefore, Friedman's proposition does not work. However, Friedman's proposition about monetary phenomena has become more global now than ever before.

> ### DO YOU KNOW?
>
> On 8 January 2022, the Central Bank of Venezuela stated that Venezuela's annual inflation rate hit 686.4 per cent in 2021, demonstrating a deceleration of consumer price growth, as opposed to the previous year when inflation was 2,959.8 per cent.
>
> *Source: The Economic Times*, 8 January 2022

Masaaki Shirakawa, the former governor of the Bank of Japan, in his Banking of International Settlement (BIS) paper, stated: 'Inflation dynamics can vary across countries and time. We should not dismiss factors unique to each country, which includes "real factors".'

He also stated in the same paper:

> Global financial conditions are becoming important as a determinant of the global economy and thus also as a determinant of the domestic economy and prices. At the same time, it is also true that each central bank is governed by the central bank law in each country. With the deepening of globalisation, however, no responsible policymaker can now dismiss the cross-border spill-overs and feedbacks of their policies.

It is very clear from these two statements why inflation may not always and everywhere be a monetary phenomenon. The above statement also beautifully describes how global financial conditions are becoming more important determinants in today's world.

Empirical Studies on the Question 'Is Inflation Always and Everywhere a Monetary Phenomenon?'

Antonella Tutino and Carlos E.J.M. Zarazaga, in Dallas Fed's 'Economic Letter, 2014', explain that in the case of Germany's hyperinflation (from 1921 to 1923),

> If the fiscal authority commits to keeping prices below a given upper bound, it could successfully convince the private sector that runaway inflation won't occur. Such a commitment implies that the government can raise the required revenue through taxes or the sale of state-owned assets. If households and businesses believe that such a fiscal policy will indeed be implemented if necessary, they will never expect inflation to spiral out of control. Thus, fiscal policy, not monetary policy, is ultimately responsible for the resulting price stabilization.

One may argue that this happened a century ago and there have been a lot of changes across the world since then. While that's true, the economy and its functions remain the same.

In 2005, a research paper on the same topic was published in the *Scandinavian Journal of Economics*. Here, the authors used a sample of about 160 countries in the last 30 years and tested the quantity theory of the relationship between money and inflation. They found that there was a strong positive relation between long-run inflation and the money growth rate. They also found that the relationship between inflation and money growth for low-inflation countries was weak. They stated that in a class of low-inflation countries, money growth and velocity changes were inversely related, and inflation and output growth seemed to be exogenously driven phenomena, mostly unrelated to the growth rate of the money stock. The researchers stated that there was a strong link between inflation and money growth, almost wholly due to the presence of high-inflation or hyperinflation countries in the sample they took for their research. They concluded that there was no evidence for this statement in relatively low-inflation environments, which happened to be a characteristic of the Economic and Monetary Union (EMU) or the European Union countries.

In 2013, a case from Nigeria on the same topic was published in the *International Journal of Business and Finance Research*, and it stated:

> This study has serious policy implications for policymakers in Nigeria and other low-income countries that have continuously based their monetary policy strategy on the premise that 'inflation is always and everywhere a monetary phenomenon'. Our result indicates that this is not true for Nigeria and that the continuous use of monetary policy tools to maintain price stability is not likely to yield the desired medium to long-term monetary policy goals.

In 2020, evidence from Nigeria on the same issue was published in the Central Bank of Nigeria's *Economic and Financial Review*, and it stated:

> This study was motivated by the need to examine the significance of the proposition that 'inflation is always and everywhere a monetary phenomenon'. Findings of the study showed that there is no sufficient statistical evidence alluding to the belief that 'inflation is always and everywhere a monetary phenomenon' is applicable

to the Nigerian economy. The findings also showed that non-monetary factors: inflation expectation, import, global oil price, exchange rate, fuel pump price and monetary policy significantly induce inflationary pressure in Nigeria. Conversely, household income (the shadow of unemployment) significantly dampens inflation while Fiscal budget and GDP moderate inflation, albeit insignificantly.

Overall, the findings submit to the dominance of structural and fiscal dynamics in the inflation equation and suboptimal management in Nigeria. This suggests the articulation and functional integration of monetary policy and non-monetary policy measures as an imperative to achieving sustainable price stability in the economy.

It has to be emphasized often that we cannot ignore the real factors of the economy. In today's world, technology, demographic trends and globalization (as mentioned before by Masaaki Shirakawa and others) do affect inflation, and these can also lead to deflation if not taken into consideration while preparing the monetary policy.

Therefore, inflation is not everywhere and always a monetary phenomenon. Many may disagree with this statement, but this is the truth in today's globalized world. With advancements in technology and digital payments, things are changing in the modern world.

Is It Applicable to India?

India's inflation is not only due to monetary phenomena, but also because of factors like supply shocks, or say supply-chain bottlenecks, unemployment, demographic trends, and such others. Most of the time in India, interest rate changes are not passed on to the public. So this statement, 'inflation is always and everywhere a monetary phenomenon', would not apply to India.

The Effectiveness of Policies and Policy Mix (or Mixed Economic Policies)

The effectiveness of any policy depends on various factors, from demographics and employment to the development of the financial system. Therefore, policymakers should always be aware of not only the prevailing conditions of the economy but also the expectations of the public, before making any policy decisions (as the RBI does for every monetary policy decision).

Policymakers should also always be aware that one policy framework alone cannot solve all the problems in the economy. For any economy, both fiscal and monetary policies should go hand in hand to address economic issues. Whatever time it may be, the mixed economic policy framework is the most effective one to handle all economic problems.

Annexures

Annexure I

Hyperinflation in History[19]	
Country Year(s)	Highest Inflation per Month (Percentage)
France 1789–96	143.26
Germany 1920–23	29,525.71
Austria 1921–22	124.27
Poland 1921–24	187.54
Soviet Union 1922–24	278.72
Hungary 1923–24	82.18
Greece 1942–45	11,288
Hungary 1945–46	1.295×10^{16}
Taiwan 1945–49	398.73
China 1947–49	4,208.73
Bolivia 1984–86	120.39
Nicaragua 1986–89	126.62
Peru 1988–90	114.12
Argentina 1989–90	196.6
Poland 1989–90	77.33

Brazil 1989–93	84.32
Yugoslavia 1990	58.82
Azerbaijan 1991–94	118.09
Congo (Zaire) 1991–94	225
Kyrgyzstan 1992	157
Serbia 1992–94	309,000,000
Ukraine 1992–94	249
Georgia 1993–94	196.72
Armenia 1993–94	438.04
Turkmenistan 1993–96	62.5
Belarus 1994	53.4
Kazakhstan 1994	57
Tajikistan 1995	78.1
Bulgaria 1997	242.7
Zimbabwe 2007–09	2,600.2*

*Zimbabwe's last official month-to-month recording of inflation by the country's Central Statistics Office, July 2008, although estimates are much higher. The official annual rate recorded for July 2008 is 231 million per cent, and the International Monetary Fund estimated the annual inflation rate for September 2008 at 489 billion per cent.

Source: Bernholz, Peter, 'Table 2.1', *Monetary Regimes and Inflation: History, Economic and Political Relationships*, Edward Elgar Publishing, Northampton, 2003.

Annexure II

Inflation Basket in Various CPI Series				
	CPI Combined	CPI-IW	CPI Agricultural Labour (CPI-AL)	CPI Rural Labor (CPI-RL)
Base Year	2012	2016	1986–87	1986–87
Weights of Major Groups				
Food, Beverages, Tobacco	48.24	48.47	72.94	70.47
Fuel and Light	6.84	6.43	8.35	7.90
Housing	10.07	15.27	–	–
Clothing and Footwear	6.53	6.57	6.98	9.76
Miscellaneous	28.32	23.26	11.73	11.87
Total	100	100	100	100
Compiling Agency	CSO	Labour Bureau, GoI		

Source: Central Statistics Office (CSO), Ministry of Statistics and Programme Implementation, Government of India (GoI); Labour Bureau, GoI

Annexure III

Wholesale Price Index—Annual Average Inflation (in %)	
Year	All Commodities
1	2
(Base: 1970–71 = 100)	
1971–72	5.6
1972–73	10.1
1973–74	20.2
1974–75	25.2
1975–76	-1.1
1976–77	2.1
1977–78	5.2
1978–79	0.1
1979–80	17.1
1980–81	18.2
1981–82	9.4
(Base: 1981–82 = 100)	
1982–83	4.9
1983–84	7.5
1984–85	6.5
1985–86	4.4

Annexure III

Wholesale Price Index—Annual Average Inflation (in %)	
Year	All Commodities
1	2
1986–87	5.8
1987–88	8.1
1988–89	7.5
1989–90	7.4
1990–91	10.3
1991–92	13.7
1992–93	10.1
1993–94	8.4
(Base: 1993–94 = 100)	
1994–95	12.6
1995–96	8.0
1996–97	4.6
1997–98	4.4
1998–99	5.9
1999–2000	3.3
2000–01	7.2
2001–02	3.6
2002–03	3.4
2003–04	5.5
2004–05	6.5
(Base: 2004–05 = 100)	
2005–06	4.5
2006–07	6.6
2007–08	4.7
2008–09	8.1

Wholesale Price Index—Annual Average Inflation (in %)	
Year	All Commodities
1	2
2009–10	3.8
2010–11	9.6
2011–12	8.9
(Base: 2011–12 = 100)	
2012–13	6.9
2013–14	5.2
2014–15	1.2
2015–16	-3.7
2016–17	1.7
2017–18	3.0
2018–19	4.3
2019–20	1.7
2020–21	1.3
2021–22	13.0
2022–23	9.4
2023–24	-07

Source: Office of the Economic Adviser, Ministry of Commerce and Industry, Government of India

Annexure IV

Month-wise Consumer Price Index (CPI) Inflation (%) From 2014 to October 2024 (Base 2012 = 100)		
Year	Month	Combined
2014	January	8.60
2014	February	7.88
2014	March	8.25
2014	April	8.48
2014	May	8.33
2014	June	6.77
2014	July	7.39
2014	August	7.03
2014	September	5.63
2014	October	4.62
2014	November	3.27
2014	December	4.28
Yearly Average		6.71
2015	January	5.19
2015	February	5.37
2015	March	5.25
2015	April	4.87
2015	May	5.01

Inflation

2015	June	5.40
2015	July	3.69
2015	August	3.74
2015	September	4.41
2015	October	5.00
2015	November	5.41
2015	December	5.61
Yearly Average		4.91
2016	January	5.69
2016	February	5.26
2016	March	4.83
2016	April	5.47
2016	May	5.76
2016	June	5.77
2016	July	6.07
2016	August	5.05
2016	September	4.39
2016	October	4.20
2016	November	3.63
2016	December	3.41
Yearly Average		4.96
2017	January	3.17
2017	February	3.65
2017	March	3.89
2017	April	2.99
2017	May	2.18
2017	June	1.46
2017	July	2.36
2017	August	3.28

Annexure IV

Year	Month	Value
2017	September	3.28
2017	October	3.58
2017	November	4.88
2017	December	5.21
Yearly Average		3.33
2018	January	5.07
2018	February	4.44
2018	March	4.28
2018	April	4.58
2018	May	4.87
2018	June	4.92
2018	July	4.17
2018	August	3.69
2018	September	3.70
2018	October	3.38
2018	November	2.33
2018	December	2.11
Yearly Average		3.96
2019	January	1.97
2019	February	2.57
2019	March	2.86
2019	April	2.99
2019	May	3.05
2019	June	3.18
2019	July	3.15
2019	August	3.28
2019	September	3.99
2019	October	4.62
2019	November	5.54

2019	December	7.35
Yearly Average		3.71
2020	January	7.59
2020	February	6.58
2020	March	5.84
2020	June	6.23
2020	July	6.73
2020	August	6.69
2020	September	7.27
2020	October	7.61
2020	November	6.93
2020	December	4.59
Yearly Average		6.43
2021	January	4.06
2021	February	5.03
2021	March	5.52
2021	April	4.23
2021	May	6.30
2021	June	6.26
2021	July	5.59
2021	August	5.30
2021	September	4.35
2021	October	4.48
2021	November	4.91
2021	December	5.66
Yearly Average		5.14
2022	January	6.01
2022	February	6.07
2022	March	6.95

Annexure IV

2022	April	7.79
2022	May	7.04
2022	June	7.01
2022	July	6.71
2022	August	7.00
2022	September	7.41
2022	October	6.77
2022	November	5.88
2022	December	5.72
Yearly Average		6.70
2023	January	6.52
2023	February	6.44
2023	March	5.66
2023	April	4.70
2023	May	4.31
2023	June	4.87
2023	July	7.44
2023	August	6.83
2023	September	5.02
2023	October	4.87
2023	November	5.55
2023	December	5.69
Yearly Average		5.66
2024	January	5.10
2024	February	5.09
2024	March	4.85
2024	April	4.83
2024	May	4.80
2024	June	5.08

2024	July	3.60
2024	August	3.65
2024	September	5.49
2024	October	6.21
2024	November	5.48
2024	December	5.22
Yearly Average		4.95

Source: CPI data from CSO website, MoSPI

Annexure V

Monetary Policy Framework and Communication in India

The Reserve Bank of India (RBI) Act of 1934 was amended in May 2016 for the implementation of a flexible inflation-targeting framework. Under Section 45ZA, along with consultation with the central government, the gazette was notified for inflation targeting. It was decided that the goalpost would be for the next five years, with an inflation target of four per cent (±2 per cent).

The RBI's monetary policy communication was clear that its policies were going to target inflation. Policy communication tools included press releases, monetary policy statements, monetary policy minutes, an increasing role of explicit forward-looking communication about the policy stance (which is normally mentioned in both minutes and statements), asset purchases, and the governor's press conference.

Analysing policy statements during flexible inflation targeting reveals a focus on words like inflation, price and growth. However, during RBI's multiple-indicators monetary policy period, these words became less significant in favour of terms like GDP, credit, money market, financial market, etc.

This shows how the RBI has changed its communication and made it clearer for consumers and investors or businesses. This helps them make their decisions more wisely.

Annexure VI

Studies of Countries

(The first seven countries that adopted inflation targeting analysed in chronological order)

New Zealand

In December 1989, the Reserve Bank of New Zealand Act (RBA) was passed and New Zealand became the first country to adopt inflation targeting. New Zealand experienced variable inflation for more than 15 years in the 1970s and the 1980s (including a fivefold rise in consumer inflation)—these disappointing economic performances were attributed to the oil shock in 1973, and the price freeze and wage distortion in the 1980s. The monetary policy was not consistent with low inflation during these periods, which explained the relatively early adoption of inflation targeting by New Zealand. As the inflation-targeting pioneer, New Zealand implemented important changes in this framework over the past decade.[20]

New Zealand's experience with inflation targeting has been positive despite the economy's inherent susceptibility to external shocks. The achievement reflects an inclination towards 'learn by doing', and also effective policy changes undertaken by the national authorities.

Canada

The federal government and the Bank of Canada jointly announced inflation targeting and targets for reducing inflation in February 1991. In the previous decade, the Canadian monetary policy was conducted without a specified path to the more long-term goals or intermediate targets. There is hardly any evidence that suggests that the inflation target announcement made any significant impact on inflation expectations. But the low realized rate of inflation from 1992 was probably the primary factor in shifting inflation expectations downwards.[21]

Canada started its inflation target at three per cent (3%) of the core consumer price inflation, and fixed the time to achieve it in December 1992. This was later reduced to two per cent (2%) in 1995. The inflation target range was later set from one per cent (1%) to three per cent (3%) till the end of 2001.

Inflation targeting in Canada endured its acid test during the global financial crisis which happened in 2007–09. This helped the Canadian economy recover fast, and also retained the public's confidence in central bank policies as the inflation target was achieved and it sailed through in spite of the extreme conditions.

The United Kingdom

A month after its exit from the exchange rate mechanism (ERM) of the European monetary system, in October 1992, the chancellor of the exchequer announced the adoption of inflation targeting as the Bank of England's (BoE) new monetary policy framework. Inflation targeting aimed to provide a new nominal anchor, along with restoring credibility. During the 1970s and 1980s, since money demand instabilities reduced the use of broad money and base money intermediate targets were ineffective, inflation targeting was never viewed as a viable alternative by the United Kingdom.

Since the introduction of the inflation-targeting framework, the United Kingdom never experienced target breaches. The improving fiscal position of the government was a reflection of the general success of inflation targeting. The government and the BoE disagreed on the monetary policy decision to be taken on many occasions when the BoE was measuring inflationary dangers to be higher than the government's estimations. When the BoE received instrument independence, the increased uncertainties and the impact of inflation expectations were eliminated. Since then, inflation expectations have been near the 2.5 per cent target.[22]

Finland

From February 1993, Finland operated an explicit inflation-targeting framework till the introduction of the single euro currency in January 1999. Inflation targeting aimed to increase the credibility of the monetary policy and to increase transparency by making more room for lowering interest rates. This was because Finland's economy was in a full-scale banking and economic crisis at the beginning of the 1990s. Due to a fall in private consumption and investment, along with the collapse of trade with former Soviet Republics, real GDP declined by three per cent a year from 1990–92. As a result, the Finnish inflation was relatively low at the onset of inflation targeting (2.6 per cent in 1992).

Sweden

On 15 January 1993, after exiting from ERM with the EU, the Central Bank of Sweden (i.e. Sveriges Riksbank) announced that it would adopt an inflation-targeting framework. After the continuous defence against several speculative attacks on Sweden's currency (i.e. the krona) in 1992, Sweden allowed its currency to float through high interest rates. Overnight, the interest rate had risen to 500 per cent, an unsustainable rate, by September 1993. Sweden was one of the pioneers to adopt inflation targeting along with its institutional features, which have evolved over time. In 1997, the initiative for the two most important changes was taken with the transparency of monetary policy and central bank independence.

The inflation-targeting system was a success in Sweden. It cemented the credibility of the monetary policy rapidly, though it was not transparent in the introductory period. The credibility of inflation targeting was enhanced by steady fiscal consolidation after its adoption. Within two years of its adoption, inflation was brought down to the target level, and remained low thereafter. Although exchange rate variability remained relatively high, the pass-through to consumer price inflation weakened, mainly because exchange rate movements were perceived to be temporary.[23]

Australia

In April 1993, Australia announced that it would implement inflation targeting to increase transparency and the credibility of the monetary policy, along with anchoring inflation expectations. This was intended to provide a nominal anchor for the monetary policy which had been missing since 1985, when the Reserve Bank of Australia (RBA) abandoned its monetary targets. The RBA had substantial flexibility in conducting its monetary policy compared to other inflation targeters. This high flexibility was necessary as the RBA pursued its monetary policy for price stability by taking into account the short-run implications for real output and employment (RBA, 1996). Since the introduction of inflation targeting, it has not imposed any restrictions on the monetary policy.

Spain

In December 1994, the Bank of Spain (BoS) announced its intention to adopt an inflation-targeting framework from January 1995, and it operated under this framework till it entered the European Economic and Monetary Union in January 1999. As required by the Maastricht Treaty on the European Union, the law on the autonomy of the BoS was one of the reasons for the decision to target inflation. The law defined price stability as the primary objective of the monetary policy, provided the BoS with instrument independence, prohibited the financing of government expenditure, and specified measures for transparency and accountability.[24] During Spain's four-year period of inflation targeting, there was a decline in inflation to the lowest level in decades. The monetary policy faced numerous challenges in its initial years. Despite the rise in central bank rates in response to inflation uncertainties, the Spanish currency (the peseta) came under speculative pressure in March 1995 and was devalued.

The Bank of Spain tightened its monetary policy till the actual inflation reached 4.3 per cent in December 1995, which strengthened its currency. Eventually, Spain's long-term interest rates fell below four per cent, and consumer inflation fell below two per cent. This made Spain eligible to become a member of the European Economic and Monetary Union.

South Africa

On 23 February 2000, South Africa (SA) formally adopted and introduced inflation targeting. The inflation target range was three to six per cent. The inflation target was for the headline consumer price index calculated by Stats SA. In 2017, the Monetary Policy Committee of South Africa emphasized that it would like to see inflation close to 4.5 per cent, the midpoint of the target range (i.e. three to six per cent).

Japan

Japan adopted a new monetary policy framework, inflation targeting, on 23 January 2013, and increased its inflation target from one to two per cent. This was an effort to put an end to the chronic deflation which Japan was facing for more than a decade. The inflation target was measured in terms of the year-on-year rate change in the headline consumer price index. Japan termed their inflation target as the price stability target.

The range of inflation rates from 2006 to 2011 was zero per cent to two per cent, with the midpoint range of one per cent. To overcome over a decade of deflation and stimulate the economy, the Bank of Japan (BoJ) announced its official target as ±2 per cent in February 2012. Since then, Japan's inflation target has remained at two per cent.

Inflation targeting was a partial success in terms of inflation, but it was successful in terms of real economic activity. There are three lessons which can be learnt from Japan's inflation targeting. These are: i) an inflation target does not guarantee any degree of increase in inflation to the target level, ii) the success of inflation targeting is also dependent on gaining the confidence of the public, and iii) consensus among policymakers will boost the confidence of the public in the central bank's policy framework.

Russia

For the first time in its history, Russia announced inflation targeting as its mid-term goal in 2006. In 2007, Russia, in its monetary policy guidelines, named price stability as well as moving towards inflation targeting as its long-term objective. Since then, moving away from the exchange rate to inflation targeting has become the primary objective of Russia's monetary policy. In its monetary policy guidelines of 2007, Russia clearly stated that they had decided to reduce the inflation rate to the range of 4 to 5.5 per cent by 2009, and for 2007, they set a target range of 6.5 to 8 per cent (year-on-year, December to December). In 2015, Russia moved to full-fledged inflation targeting as the primary objective of its monetary policy. It set an inflation target of four per cent.

Source: 'Adopting Inflation Targeting: Practical Issues for Emerging Market Countries', by Andrea Schaechter, Mark R. Stone, and Mark Zelmer (2000)

Annexure VII

The History of Central Banking in India

In 1773, during British rule, the governor of Bengal recommended the establishment of a general bank in Bengal and Bihar; it was short-lived though. In 1914, the Chamberlain Commission included a comprehensive memorandum prepared by John Maynard Keynes (one of the members), proposing the merger of three presidency banks into one central bank which was to be named the Imperial Bank of India. By the end of the First World War, it became apparent that a central banking institution was needed. In 1920 the Imperial Bank Act was passed, and the merger finally took place in 1921. The Imperial Bank was a commercial bank which performed certain central banking functions like being a bankers' bank and a banker to the government. At the time, the core banking function of issuing currency notes and the management of foreign currency was the responsibility of the central government. At the time, central banking theory was established on the basis of the notion that it was unsuitable for a commercial bank to function as the central bank in a country.

In 1926, the Royal Commission on Indian Currency and Finance (the Hilton Young Commission) recommended that the separate functions and divisions of responsibilities for the control of currency and credit should be abolished. It suggested the establishment of a central bank which would be named the Reserve Bank of India. This was considered necessary to boost banking facilities all over the country.

In January 1927, a bill to establish the Reserve Bank of India was introduced in the Legislative Assembly. This bill was dropped due to differences in views regarding ownership, the composition of the board of directors, and the Constitution. In 1933, a white paper on Indian constitutional reforms proposed the setting up of the Reserve Bank of India which would be free from political influences.

In 1931, the Indian Central Banking Enquiry Committee strongly recommended the establishment of the Reserve Bank of India. All these events led to the introduction of a new bill in 1933, which was passed in 1934, and finally, the RBI Act came into effect on 1 January 1935. The RBI was inaugurated on 1 April 1935.

Source: Adapted from the *Report on Currency and Finance, 2004–05* [which mentioned the source as RBI (1970)]

Annexure VIII

The Evolution of Monetary Policies Transmission Mechanism in India

Over the years, the monetary policy in India has changed continuously and responded to both global and domestic macroeconomic conditions. The procedure of operations has undergone substantial changes over the past 70 years. There were no formal monetary policy objectives, instruments or transmission channels before the mid-1980s. There was only the administering of supply or allocation, and the demand for credit with the alignment of the Five-Year Plan.

From 1985 to 1997, broad money (M3) emerged as the nominal anchor based on the premise of a stable relationship between money, output and prices. This was called flexible monetary targeting with feedback. In this approach, the broad money (M3) was projected with the expected GDP growth and a tolerable level of inflation. Reserve money was used as the operating target and bank reserves as the operating instruments in the determination of both interest rates and exchange rates.

This framework underwent changes over the late 1990s as interest rates and exchange rates gained importance in the transmission mechanism of the monetary policy. India switched over to the multiple indicator approach in 1998–99. During this period, the CRR was brought down to 4.5 per cent from a peak of 15 per cent in 1994–95, and the SLR was brought down to 18 per cent in 2022 (it was reduced from 38.5 per cent in 1992).

The MIA framework provided the necessary flexibility to the RBI. Using this approach, the RBI responded more effectively to the changes which took place in domestic financial markets and international economic conditions.

The reforms in the monetary policy operating framework—initiated in the late 1980s—came in the form of the LAF in 2000. According to the LAF, the RBI was supposed to set its policy rates—the repo and the reverse repo rates—for operations, thereby providing a corridor for overnight money market rates. These rates are the nominal anchor, even at present.

Source: Adapted from *The Report on Currency and Finance, 2004–05*

Glossary

Aggregate Demand
: Aggregate demand is the sum total of the components of spending in the economy, added to get the GDP: Y = C + I + G + X − M. It is the total amount of demand for (or expenditure on) goods and services produced in the economy.

Aggregate Output/Supply
: Aggregate output is the total output in an economy, across all sectors and regions.

Bank Rate
: Bank rate is the rate at which the Reserve Bank is ready to buy or rediscount bills of exchange or other commercial papers.

Broad Money
: This is the measure of the money supply in an economy with broad coverage. Broad money usually includes national currency and deposits held by residents in depository institutions; these deposits may be either transferable, such as demand deposits, or non-transferable, such as term deposits; deposits denominated in foreign currency and held by residents may also be included in broad money.

Budget
: This is an annual financial statement that represents anticipated expenditure and expected revenue generation in a particular fiscal year.

Cash Reserve Ratio (CRR)
: CRR is the cash parked by banks in their specified current accounts maintained with the RBI.

Certificates of Deposits (CDs)	A certificate of deposit is a savings account that earns an interest rate for a fixed period of time (say, six months or a year and so on). CDs usually earn more interest rates than savings accounts. CDs are better known as term or fixed deposits.
Central Bank	A central bank is the only bank which can create or issue currencies—usually, it is a part of the government. Its key functions are issuing currency and regulating the supply of credit in the economy.
Constant Prices	These are prices which are adjusted to inflation or deflation.
Current Prices	These are nominal prices. In other words, they are influenced by the effect of price inflation or deflation.
Deflation	This is when the inflation rate is negative, i.e. prices are falling on average rather than rising at all. If prices in the basket of goods and services used to measure changes in the cost of living are falling at two per cent on average, it would be deflation.
Disinflation	This is a condition when the rate of inflation is falling but is still above zero.
Economic Growth	This refers to an increase in the capacity of an economy to produce goods and services, compared from one period of time to another.
Expectations of Inflation (or) Inflation Expectations	These refer to the expected or anticipated value of the rate of inflation for some specified future period.
Financial Year	The financial year is the 12-monthly periods of budget and accounts of the government. The financial year runs from 1 April to 31 March.
Fiscal Dominance	This is a situation when there is unsustainable financing of fiscal deficit which becomes a major source of inflation and macroeconomic instability.
Fiscal Policy	The fiscal policy is a set of decisions a government makes with respect to taxation, spending and borrowing.

Gross Domestic Product (GDP)	The GDP is an increase in the total amount of goods and services produced in the country over a period of time, normally one year. It is also defined as a measure of total national output, income and expenditure in the economy.
Hedge/ Hedging	Hedging is a financial strategy to lessen the risks in financial assets. It is an investment to reduce the risk of adverse price movements in an asset or security.
Hyperinflation	Hyperinflation is when a country experiences extraordinarily high rates of inflation—for example, more than 50 per cent per month. This often leads to a loss of faith in the currency and a highly costly breakdown in the country's ability to carry out its day-to-day economic transactions.
Index	An index is a measure of the amount of something in one period of time, compared to the amount of the same thing in a different period of time, called the reference period or base period. It is common to set its value at 100 in the reference period.
Inflation	Inflation is the rate of change of some general index of prices. In many countries, it is common to use an index based on a collection of prices of consumer goods—such as the consumer price index (CPI). The measure of CPI inflation is then the rate of change in the CPI.
Inflation Targeting	Inflation targeting is a monetary policy regime where the central bank changes interest rates to influence the aggregate demand in order to keep the economy close to an inflation target, which is normally specified by the government.
Interest	Interest refers to the scheduled payments made to a creditor in return for the use of borrowed money, and is determined by the interest rate, the amount borrowed (principal), and the duration of the loan.
Interest Rate	The interest rate is the fixed charge or return on a financial asset, usually expressed on an annual basis. It is expressed as a percentage of the price of the asset.

International Monetary Fund (IMF)	The IMF is an international organization with 190 members. It was formed in 1944 from the Bretton Woods Agreement mainly to promote monetary cooperation among its members. Its statutory purposes include promoting the balanced growth of international trade, stability of exchange rates, and the maintenance of orderly exchange arrangements among members. The IMF monitors global economic and financial developments, gives policy advice, lends to member countries with balance of payments problems, and provides technical assistance in its areas of expertise.
Keynesian Economics	Keynesian economics refers to the followers of Keynes's theory—a theory formulated by John Maynard Keynes, a British economist.
Liquidity Adjustment Facility (LAF)	The LAF enables the RBI to modulate short-term liquidity under varied financial market conditions to ensure stable conditions in the overnight (call) money market. The LAF operates through daily repo and reverse repo auctions, thereby setting a corridor for the short-term interest rate consistent with policy objectives.
Liquidity Trap	This is a situation where expansionary monetary policy fails. Despite the fall of (or zero) interest rates, people tend to save more rather than spend.
Monetary Policy	The monetary policy is a set of decisions a government makes, usually through its central bank, regarding the amount of money in circulation in the economy.
Money	Money is anything that is generally accepted in exchange as payment for goods and services. While the key function of money is to act as a medium of exchange, it also serves as a store of value, unit of account, and standard of deferred payment.
Money Supply	Money supply is the amount of money in circulation (includes coins, paper or currency notes, and other liquid instruments).

Nominal Anchor	Nominal anchor is the policy objective or goal of monetary policy.
Nominal Interest Rates	Nominal interest rates are the interest rates that you earn (or pay) on a loan; this is unadjusted to the inflation rate.
Open Market Operations (OMO)	OMO is the purchase and sale of government securities to inject or take out money into/from the economy. The purchases inject money into the economy to stimulate growth, and the sales do the reverse.
Quantitative Easing (QE)	QE is an unconventional monetary policy strategy used by central banks to increase the money supply and to keep the credit flowing to the economy. This is done to stimulate the economy.
Real GDP	Real GDP is GDP (gross domestic product) adjusted for inflation. Real GDP provides the value of GDP in constant prices, which is used as an indicator of the volume of the nation's output.
Real Interest Rates	Real interest rates are nominal interest rates minus actual or expected inflation rate. In other words, they are inflation-adjusted interest rates.
Recession	Recession refers to a significant reduction in economic activity over the period of time. In other words, it is a reduction in real GDP (output), and this is accompanied by a significant rise in the unemployment rate.
Repo Rate	Repo rate is the interest rate (fixed) at which the Reserve Bank provides liquidity to all commercial banks, against the collateral of government and other approved securities.
Reverse Repo Rate	Reverse repo rate is the (fixed) interest rate at which the RBI absorbs liquidity on an overnight basis from banks, against the collateral of eligible government securities under the LAF.
Stagflation	Stagflation is a combination of high inflation and economic stagnation.

Statutory Liquidity Ratio (SLR)	The statutory liquidity ratio is in the form of cash (book value), gold (current market value), and balances in unencumbered approved securities.
Supply Shock	A supply shock is an unexpected change on the supply side of the economy, such as a rise or fall in oil prices, or an improvement in technology.
Transmission Mechanism	This is the complex chain of cause and effect that connects the central bank's policy instrument (typically the setting of a short-term interest rate) with asset prices, aggregate demand, total output, the output gap, and eventually inflation.
Unemployment	This is a situation in which a person who is able and willing to work is not employed.
Velocity of Money	The velocity of money is a measure which expresses the number of times the average unit of currency is used to purchase goods and services within a given time period in an economy.
Wage-Push Inflation	The inflation that occurs due to an increase in wages is called wage-push inflation; wage increase can cause the prices of final products to increase.

Acknowledgements

I am indebted to God for his constant help. I express my gratitude to Mr S. Prakash, who encouraged me to write this book at the earliest. I thank my late grandmother, my mother and my uncle for their support in completing this book. I sincerely thank the editor and publisher of this book, and Rupa Publications, for their trust, professional guidance, and constant support in bringing this book to life.

Endnotes

1. Core inflation is the change in the costs of goods and services, excluding the food and energy sectors because their prices are much more volatile.
2. Johnston, Matthew, 'Worst Cases of Hyperinflation in History', *Investopedia*, 15 March 2024, https://tinyurl.com/3xmprjn4. Accessed on 21 November 2024.
3. Globalization and Monetary Policy Institute, 'Annual Report', 2011, https://tinyurl.com/3ckp76a4. Accessed on 20 January 2025.
4. Ransom, Roger L., 'The Economics of the Civil War', *EH.net*, 24 August 2001, https://tinyurl.com/3pjj4m2k. Accessed on 21 November 2024.
5. 'Inflation in the Confederacy', *Encyclopedia.com*, https://tinyurl.com/yf5pmp3s. Accessed on 21 November 2024.
6. The loans of the country's banks increased by $12 billion from 31 May 1950 to 30 May 1951. The bank issued some $6 billion by the end of January 1951. Readers of economics may refer to *What You Should Know about Inflation* by Henry Hazlitt for further reading.
7. A liquidity trap is a situation where the central bank's expansionary monetary policy fails. Despite this fall or the zero interest rates, people tend to save more, rather than spend.
8. Stockman, Alan C., 'Anticipated inflation and the capital stock in a cash in-advance economy', *Journal of Monetary Economics*, Vol. 8, No. 3, 1981, pp. 387–93, https://tinyurl.com/4jyknh8j. Accessed on 14 January 2025.
9. Phillips, A.W., 'The Relation Between Unemployment and the Rate of Change of Money Wage Rates in the United Kingdom, 1861–1957', *Economica*, Vol. 25, 1958, pp. 283–299, https://tinyurl.com/4a8p74hr. Accessed on 21 November 2024.

10 Independent Evaluation Office of the IMF, 'The IMF and Aid to Sub-Saharan Africa Evaluation Report', 2007, p. 10, https://tinyurl.com/y63f5rf6. Accessed on 23 January 2025.
11 Bierman, Harold, 'The 1929 Stock Market Crash', Economic History Association, https://tinyurl.com/c897ay7m. Accessed on 21 November 2024.
12 Primary deficit is a deficit without interest rates
13 Nominal GDP is GDP with inflation.
14 Rangarajan, C., and R.R. Arif, 'Money, Output and Prices—A Macro Econometric Model', *Economic and Political Weekly*, Vol. 25, No. 16, 1990, https://tinyurl.com/mwfykyrz. Accessed on 28 August 2022.
15 Hall, Thomas E. and William R. Hart, 'The Samuelson-Solow Phillips Curve and the Great Inflation', *History of Economics Review*, Vol. 55, No. 1, 2012, pp. 62–72, https://tinyurl.com/mbyk6utf. Accessed on 21 November 2024.
16 Gali, Jordi, and Mark Gertler, 'Inflation Dynamics: A Structural Econometric Analysis', *Journal of Monetary Economics*, Vol. 44, No. 2, 1999, pp. 195–222.
17 'Organisation and Functions', *Reserve Bank of India for Common Person*, Reserve Bank of India, https://tinyurl.com/ycxhzcru. Accessed on 21 November 2024.
18 *Labour Bureau*, https://tinyurl.com/yxwhpm77. Accessed on 13 February, 2025; *Ministry of Statistics and Programme Implementation*, https://tinyurl.com/bv6k7wy2. Accesses on 13 February, 2025.
19 Bernholz, Peter, 'Table 2.1', *Monetary Regimes and Inflation: History, Economic and Political Relationships*, Edward Elgar Publishing, Northampton, 2003.
20 Bernanke, Ben S., et al., *Inflation Targeting: Lessons from the International Experience*, Princeton University Press, Princeton, 1999; Sherwin, Murray, 'Strategic Choices in Inflation Targeting: The New Zealand Experience', *Inflation Targeting in Practice: Strategic and Operational Issues and Application to Emerging Market Economies*, Mario I. Blejer, et al. (eds.), International Monetary Fund, Washington, 2000.
21 Thiessen, Gordon G., 'The Canadian Experience with Targets for Inflation Control', Gibson Lecture at Queen's University, Kingston, October 1998.
22 Haldane, Andrew, 'Targeting Inflation: The U.K. in Retrospect',

Inflation Targeting in Practice: Strategic and Operational Issues and Application to Emerging Market Economies, Mario I. Blejer, et al., (eds.), International Monetary Fund, Washington, 2000.

23. Berg, Claes, 'Inflation Forecast Targeting: The Swedish Experience', *Sveriges Riksbank Quarterly Review*, Vol. 3, 1999, pp. 44–70.
24. Gutiérrez, Fernando, 'Monetary Policy Following the Law on the Autonomy of the Banco de Espana', *Monetary Policy and Inflation in Spain*, José Luis Malo de Molina, Josá Viñals, and Fernando Gutiérrez (eds.), St. Martin's Press, New York, 1998.

Bibliography

Achua, J.K., H. Nagado, and I.I. Okafor, 'Is Inflation Always and Everywhere a Monetary Phenomenon? Evidence from Nigeria', Central Bank of Nigeria, *Economic and Financial Review*, Vol. 58, No. 1, March 2020, pp. 81–101.

Alcidi, C., D. Gros, and F. Shamsfakhr, 'Inflation Expectations: Models and Measures', *Publication for the Committee on Economic and Monetary Affairs*, Policy Department for Economic, Scientific and Quality of Life Policies, European Parliament, 2022.

Ang, James S., Jess H. Chua, and Anand S. Desai, 'Evidence That The Common Stock Market Adjusts Fully For Expected Inflation', *The Journal of Financial Research*, Vol. 2, No. 2, 1979, pp. 97–109.

Arbuckle, Alex Q., '1922–1923: Hyperinflation in Germany', *Mashable.com*, https://tinyurl.com/msfvh6sf. Accessed on 21 November 2024.

Backhouse, Fid, et al., 'Hyperinflation in the Weimar Republic', *Britannica*, 19 February 2024, https://tinyurl.com/3jb9k87y. Accessed on 21 November 2024.

Barro, Robert J., 'Inflation and Economic Growth', *Annals of Economics and Finance*, Society for AEF, Vol. 14, No. 1, 2013, pp. 121–44.

Benes, Jaromir, et al., 'Inflation-Forecast Targeting for India: An Outline of the Analytical Framework', IMF Working paper, WP/17/32, International Monetary Fund, 2017, https://tinyurl.com/mrxyhc3x. Accessed on 21 January 2025.

Bierman, Harold, 'The 1929 Stock Market Crash', *EH.Net*, 26 March 2008, https://tinyurl.com/c897ay7m. Accessed on 21 November 2024.

Boyd, John, Ross Levine, and Bruce Smith, 'The Impact of Inflation on Financial Sector Performance', *Journal of Monetary Economics*,

Vol. 47, 2001, pp. 221–48, https://tinyurl.com/39uvcvup. Accessed on 21 November 2024.

Brouwer, Gordon de, and Luci Ellis, 'Forward-looking Behaviour and Credibility: Some Evidence and Implications for Policy', RBA Research Discussion Papers rdp9803, Reserve Bank of Australia, 1998.

Cedrom, 'BCV admite hiperinflación de 53.798.500% desde 2016', *Venezuela al Dia*, 28 May 2019, https://tinyurl.com/yck48x6a. Accessed on 21 November 2024.

Central Statistics Office (CSO), Ministry of Statistics and Programme Implementation, Government of India; Labour Bureau, Government of India.

'Consumidor', Banco Central De Venezuela, https://tinyurl.com/2ftunw8z. Accessed on 21 November 2024.

'CPI Rural Urban Manual and SBI Ecowrap', No. 68, FY20, 21 January 2020.

De Grauwe, Paul, and Magdalena Polan, 'Is Inflation Always and Everywhere a Monetary Phenomenon?', *Scandinavian Journal of Economics*, Vol. 107, No. 2, June 2005, pp. 239–59.

Debelle, Guy, Paul Masson, Miguel Savastano, and Sunil Sharma, 'Inflation Targeting as a Framework for Monetary Policy', *IMF Economic Issues*, No. 15, October 1998.

Doyin, Salami, 'Nigeria Kelikume Ikechukwu, Is inflation always and everywhere a monetary phenomenon? The case of Nigeria', *The International Journal of Business and Finance Research*, Vol. 7, No. 2, 2013, pp. 105–14.

Easterly, William, and Michael Bruno, 'Inflation Crises and Long-Run Growth', Policy Research Working Paper, The World Bank, 1995.

Feldstein, Martin, *Inflation and Stock Market in Tax Rules, and Capital Formation*, University of Chicago Press, Chicago, 1983.

Fernando, Jason, 'Inflation: What It Is and How to Control Inflation Rates', *Investopedia*, 7 November 2024, https://tinyurl.com/mr25u9zv. Accessed on 20 January 2025.

Fischer, S., 'The Role of Macroeconomic Factors in Growth', NBER Working Paper, No. 4565, 1993.

Fisher, Irving, and Harry G. Brown, 'The Equation of Exchanges', *The Purchasing Power of Money: Its Determination and Relation to Credit, Interest and Crises*, New and revised edition, Augustus M. Kelly

Publishers, New York, 1911, pp. 8–32.

Fisher, Irving, *The Stock Market Crash and After*, Macmillan, New York, 1930.

Freedman, Charles, and Douglas Laxton, 'Why Inflation Targeting?' IMF Working Papers 2009/086, International Monetary Fund, 2009.

Friedman, Milton, 'The Optimum Quantity of Money', *The Optimum Quantity of Money and Other Essays*, Aldine Publishing Company, United Kingdom, 1969, pp. 51–67.

Friedman, Milton, 'The Role of Monetary Policy', *American Economic Review*, Vol. LVIII, No. 1, March 1968, pp. 1–17.

Ghosh, A., and S. Phillips, 'Warning: Inflation may be harmful to your Growth', IMF Working Papers, Vol. 45, No. 4, International Monetary Fund, 1998.

Globalization and Monetary Policy Institute, '2011 Annual Report', February 2012, https://tinyurl.com/2vn4x7em. Accessed on 21 November 2024.

Ha, Jongrim, et al., 'What Explains Global Inflation', *IMF Economic Review*, 2024, https://tinyurl.com/mr3a7pr8. Accessed on 21 November 2024.

Ha, Jongrim, M. Ayhan Kose, and Franziska Ohnsorge, 'Inflation in Emerging and Developing Economies: Evolution, Drivers, and Policies', World Bank, https://tinyurl.com/2tb2k8u7. Accessed on 14 January 2025.

Hall, T.E., and W.R. Hart, 'The Samuelson-Solow "Phillips Curve" and the Great Inflation', 2010, Miami University Farmer School of Business, Working Paper.

Hanke, Steve H., and Alex K.F. Kwok, 'On the Measurement of Zimbabwe's Hyperinflation', *Cato Journal*, Vol. 29, 2009, pp. 353–64.

Hazlitt, Henry, *Man vs. The Welfare State*, Arlington House, Ludwig von Mises Institute, 1970.

——*What You Should Know About Inflation*, Second Edition, D. Van Nostrand Company, Princeton, 1964.

Independent Evaluation Office of the IMF, 'The IMF and Aid to Sub-Saharan Africa Evaluation Report', 2007, https://tinyurl.com/y63f5rf6. Accessed on 23 January 2025.

'Inflation in the Confederacy', *Encyclopedia.com*, 27 October 2022, https://tinyurl.com/yf5pmp3s. Accessed on 21 November 2021.

Jahan, Sarwat, 'Inflation Targeting: Holding the Line', *Finance and*

Development, 2012, https://tinyurl.com/2yz987bb. Accessed on 21 January 2025.

Johnston, Matthew, 'Worst Cases of Hyperinflation', *Investopedia*, 15 March 2024, https://tinyurl.com/bdh6vsr3. Accessed on 21 November 2024.

Mallik, Girijasankar, and Anis Chowdhury, 'Effect of inflation uncertainty, output uncertainty and oil price on inflation and growth in Australia', *Journal of Economic Studies*, Vol. 38, No. 4, 2011, pp. 414–29.

Ministry of Labour & Employment, Government of India, 'Report on New Series of Consumer Price Index for Industrial Workers (CPI-IW) (Base 2016 = 100)', 2020, https://tinyurl.com/3bkcynkk. Accessed on 21 November 2024.

Mishkin, Frederic S., 'The Causes and Propagation of Financial Instability: Lessons for Policymakers', Proceedings, Economic Policy Symposium, Federal Reserve Bank of Kansas City, 1997, pp. 55–96, https://tinyurl.com/5n7pc9kp. Accessed on 20 January 2025.

Mohanty, D., 'Monetary policy framework in India: Experience with multiple-indicators approach', Speech delivered at the Conference of the Orissa Economic Association in Baripada, Orissa on 21 February 2010.

'Monetary Policy and Central Bank Communication', Address by Shri Shaktikanta Das, Governor, Reserve Bank of India, delivered at the National Defence College, Ministry of Defence, Government of India, 4 March 2022.

'Monetary Policy in Developing Countries', *Money and Economic Development: The Horowitz Lectures of 1972*, Praeger, New York, 1973, pp. 38–67.

Montevirgen, Karl, 'Inflation', *Britannica*, 11 November 2024, https://tinyurl.com/5n7tc4nm. Accessed on 21 November 2024.

Motley, Brian, 'Growth and inflation: a cross-country study', Working Papers in Applied Economic Theory 94-08, Federal Reserve Bank of San Francisco, 1994.

Nakata, Taisuke, 'Raising the Inflation Target: Lessons from Japan', *Federal Reserve*, 8 January 2020, https://tinyurl.com/r78suk8k. Accessed on 21 November 2024.

Nogaro, Bertrand, 'Hungary's Recent Monetary Crisis and Its Theoretical Meaning', *The American Economic Review*, Vol. 38, No. 4, 1948, pp. 526–42.

Oner, Ceyda, 'Inflation: Prices on the Rise', International Monetary

Fund, Finance and Development, 2012, https://tinyurl.com/vzervpbw. Accessed on 18 January 2025.

'Organisation and Functions', *Reserve Bank of India for Common Person*, Reserve Bank of India, https://tinyurl.com/2huu8z8f. Accessed on 27 January 2025.

Pettinger, Tejvan, 'Different types of inflation', *Economicshelp.org*, 4 April 2021, https://tinyurl.com/r2uf8f3h. Accessed on 20 January 2025.

——'Methods to Control Inflation', *Economicshelp.org*, 8 July 2022, https://tinyurl.com/4n2rnm4t. Accessed on 21 January 2025.

Phillips, A.W., 'The Relation Between Unemployment and the Rate of Change of Money Wage Rates in the United Kingdom, 1861–1957', *Economica*, Vol. 25, 1958, pp. 283–99, https://tinyurl.com/4a8p74hr. Accessed on 21 November 2024.

Ransom, Roger L., 'Economics of the Civil War', *EH.Net Encyclopedia*, 24 August 2001, https://tinyurl.com/byypub3f. Accessed on 21 November 2024.

Reddy, Y.V., 'Monetary policy operating procedures in India', Bank of International Settlements (BIS), Policy Paper No. 5, 1999, pp. 99–109.

Reserve Bank of India, 'Annual Report, 1974-75', https://tinyurl.com/2s4e39ux. Accessed on 21 November 2024.

Reserve Bank of India, 'Central Banking in India', *Report on Currency and Finance, 2004-05*, 2005–06, pp. 95–121.

Samantaraya, Amaresh, and R.K. Pattnaik, 'Indian Experience of Inflation: A Review of the Evolving Process', *Economic and Political Weekly*, Vol. 41, No. 4, 2006, pp. 349–56.

Schaechter, Andrea, Mark R. Stone, and Mark Zelman, 'Adopting Inflation Targeting: Practical Issues for Emerging Market Countries', Occasional Paper, No. 202, IMF, Washington, D.C., 2000.

Schafer, Jeffrey, 'Inflation Expectations and Their Formation: Working Paper 2022-03', Working Papers 57398, Congressional Budget Office, 2022.

Sellin, Peter, 'Monetary Policy and the Stock Market: Theory and Empirical Evidence', Sveriges Riksbank Working Paper Series, No. 72, Sveriges Riksbank, 1998.

Shirakawa, Masaaki, 'Is inflation (or deflation) "always and everywhere" a monetary phenomenon?', Bank for International Settlements (BIS), Paper 77, 31 March 2014, https://tinyurl.com/29he58hk. Accessed on 21 November 2024.

Siklos, P.L., *War Finance, Reconstruction, Hyperinflation and Stabilization in Hungary, 1938–48*, Palgrave Macmillan, London, 1991, https://tinyurl.com/mr4cn2zv. Accessed on 21 November 2024.

Stockman, Alan C., 'Anticipated Inflation and the Capital Stock in a Cash-in-Advance Economy', *Journal of Monetary Economics*, Vol. 8, 1981, pp. 387–93.

Stulz, René M., 'Asset Pricing and Expected Inflation', 1985, Alfred P. Sloan School of Management, Massachusetts Institute of Technology, Working Paper #1706-85.

Taylor, Bryan, 'The Worst Hyperinflations in History: Hungary', *Global Financial Data*, 16 April 2014, https://tinyurl.com/53hatckr. Accessed on 21 November 2024.

Tiwari, Brajesh Kumar, 'Rupee depreciated 20-fold since independence; here's how "Make in India" may boost Indian currency', *Financial Express*, 6 June 2022, https://tinyurl.com/bdhjzem9. Accessed on 21 January 2025.

Yadav, Chetan, Sameer Lama, and Rajan Gahlot, 'The Study of Inflation and Stock Market Returns in Japan', *International Journal for Research in Management and Pharmacy*, Vol. 3, No. 8, 2014, pp. 1–8, https://tinyurl.com/3nxwddpj. Accessed on 28 January 2025.

Index

aggregate demand (AD), 7, 9, 13, 15, 16, 17, 21, 40, 72, 73, 171, 174
aggregate supply (AS), 15, 16, 21, 40, 72, 73

built-in inflation, x, 14, 17

cash reserve ratio (CRR), 70, 83, 120, 123, 125, 168, 169
consumer price index (CPI), 22, 23, 24, 78, 79, 80, 86, 87, 121, 128, 145, 149, 154, 171, 180, 182
core inflation, 3, 23, 80, 176
cost-push inflation, x, 12, 14, 15
CPI Agricultural Labourers (CPI-AL), 79, 145
CPI Combined, 78, 86, 87, 121, 145
CPI Rural, 78, 79, 145, 180
CPI Rural Labourers (CPI-RL), 79, 145
CPI Urban, 78, 79

deflation, x, 20, 41, 42, 48, 138, 163, 170, 183

demand-pull inflation, x, 7, 12, 14, 16, 17

exchange rate, 12, 28, 108, 115, 123, 125, 138, 159, 161, 164

fiscal policy, xi, 35, 61, 63, 64, 65, 66, 67, 73, 83, 101, 134, 136, 170
Friedman, Milton, xii, 6, 25, 42, 49, 94, 130, 132, 133

government expenditure, 66, 67, 71, 71, 93, 162

hyperinflation, x, 14, 19, 27, 28, 30, 31, 33, 34, 35, 36, 58, 63, 67, 70, 71, 136, 137

inflation expectation, x, xi, 12, 16, 17, 48, 55, 65, 89, 90, 91, 92, 93, 94, 97, 98, 99, 100, 101, 102, 103, 104, 105, 109, 112, 113, 126, 127, 128, 158, 159, 161
inflation targeting, 92, 100, 106, 107, 108, 109, 110, 113, 114, 116, 117, 121, 122, 127, 128,

164, 171, 180, 181, 183
Keynes, J.M., 7, 40, 63, 93, 96, 165, 172

liquidity adjustment facility (LAF), 123, 124, 168, 172, 173

monetary policy, xi, xii, 8, 11, 30, 51, 64, 65, 66, 67, 71, 73, 89, 91, 92, 94, 96, 97, 100, 101, 102, 103, 106, 107, 108, 109, 110, 111, 113, 115, 117, 118, 119, 120, 121, 122, 123, 124, 126, 127, 128, 130, 131, 132, 133, 134, 136, 137, 138, 139, 155, 157, 158, 159, 160, 161, 162, 163, 164, 167, 168, 171, 172, 173
monetization, 31, 83, 85
money inflation, 34, 35, 36

open market operations (OMO), 70, 118, 173

Phillips, A.W., 44

Phillips curve, 39, 43, 44, 45, 93, 94, 95, 97
price inflation, xi, 23, 25, 26, 27, 35, 36, 37, 77, 78, 80, 93, 158, 161, 170

Quantity theory of money, 6, 40, 42, 132

repo rate, 124, 168, 173
Reserve Bank of India (RBI), 83, 117, 118, 119, 120, 121, 122, 123, 124, 125, 126, 128, 129, 139, 155, 156, 166, 168, 169, 172, 173
reverse repo rate, 173

stagflation, 14, 17, 44, 173
statutory liquidity ratio (SLR), 120, 123, 125, 168, 174
stock market, xi, 51, 52, 53, 54, 55, 56, 57, 58, 59, 60, 93

wholesale price index (WPI), 22, 80, 84, 86